It's Time

Passing Revival on to the Next Generation

Richard Crisco

Revival Press

An Imprint of
Destiny Image® Publishers, Inc.
P.O. Box 310
Shippensburg, PA 17257-0310

ISBN 1-56043-690-5

For Worldwide Distribution
Printed in the U.S.A.

Second Printing: 1997   Third Printing: 1998

This book and all other Destiny Image, Revival Press, and Treasure House books are available at Christian bookstores and distributors worldwide.

For a U.S. bookstore nearest you, call **1-800-722-6774**.
For more information on foreign distributors, call **717-532-3040**.
Or reach us on the Internet: **http://www.reapernet.com**

Check out the Brownsville website:
http://www.brownsville-revival.org

Dedication

I would like to dedicate this book:

To my heroes, the youth at Brownsville Assembly. I've never met so many teenagers who were truly on fire for Jesus like the teens the Lord has blessed me with at Brownsville. Without them, I would have no story.

To my youth leaders, who have done marvelous work in loving, caring, and nurturing our teens in close discipleship. Without them, I could never carry the load of ministry.

To my precious wife, Jane, and children, Ashley and Caleb, who have sacrificially given for the work of the ministry and love this revival.

To my best friend, Jesus. Without Him, not only would I not have a story, but I wouldn't have a life!

Contents

Foreword

Revelation From God's Heart

I love a mystery. I love to see the plot unravel and to observe what was once obscure become distinct. That is the way I would describe the Brownsville Outpouring of 1995 that continues until this day. I have had the privilege of watching from the sidelines the Holy Spirit at work, and it has been a mystery. It has always touched me how Ruth wound up in Boaz's field. All you can say is, "That's God!"

When Richard Crisco came to Brownsville to become part of our pastoral staff, it was God! God took a former Catholic and obscure youth minister and brought him into his provision. I remember the first time Richard shared with me the truth that the Holy Spirit revealed to him concerning "time." It made such an impact on his life that I knew God would give him a way to share these truths. That is what *It's Time* is all about. Richard Crisco loves the move of God. I remember that before revival broke out, he and I would talk of revival and the things of God in these last days, and I never saw greater hunger in any man. I have never met anyone, including present or former staff members, who loves to worship God more than Richard does, and he does it so unashamedly. A worshiper always gets the revelation from God's heart. As you read Richard's heart, you too will say, *it's time.*

John A. Kilpatrick, Pastor
Brownsville Assembly of God Church

Introduction

This Is the Generation

On my desk is a photo album which contains pictures of my all kids, right up to the ones who came last week. I love my kids. Three times a week I pray for each one of them by name.

One morning a few years ago as I was looking at their pictures and praying, the Lord dropped Psalm 24:6 into my heart: "...this is the generation of those who will seek Him, who will seek His face."

In the recent past, the Church has done a lot of seeking; but much of that seeking has been for God's *hand*, and not for His face. Christians have sought the Lord only for what He could do for them and how He could bless them. I felt God say to me that morning, "This generation is going to go beyond that. They are going to rise up and seek Me for who I am. They will seek My face."

And that is what we are seeing here at Brownsville Assembly of God in Pensacola, Florida. We are seeing young people who are seeking His face. This generation is the most abused, neglected, and misunderstood generation in the history of mankind. Hopelessness has gripped their hearts. When you bring that kind of people in contact with Life, they explode. They explode into worship; they explode into love and adoration for God. He is the One they have been searching for.

Throughout history, God has always had a champion in the making. At the right time that champion has stepped forward to destroy the enemy. I believe that this present generation is the greatest hope that America has. They have been tossed aside and unfairly labeled "Generation X," but God calls them a Generation of Champions. And it is time. It is time for God's hidden champions to step forward and destroy the powers of darkness.

It's time.

Chapter 1

What Time Is It?

Two weeks before Father's Day 1995 we were driving down a barren stretch of Interstate 10 between Mobile, Alabama, and Pensacola, Florida. It was 1:00 Sunday morning and the voices of my group of teenagers had grown silent. They had been praying almost nonstop for the past 33 hours. With a smile I said to my wife, "I think they finally ran out of gas."

I will never forget what happened next as long as I live. I turned on the dome light and looked into the rearview mirror, expecting to see them all fast asleep. There were still six teenagers sitting there with their hands lifted and tears streaming down their faces; their lips were moving quietly in the darkness. At that very moment, the fear of God hit me like I've never had it hit me before in my life.

Dear God! I thought to myself, *What is happening?*

The reputation of the teenagers of Brownsville Assembly was not one of praying and seeking God. In fact, in the West Florida district our youth group was known for being snobs. And they didn't like me. They made fun of me and called me a country hick. (I suppose it didn't help when I said things like, "That really cranks my tractor!") For the first two and a half years I thought I was going to die. I resigned every Wednesday night, went home and repented, and went back to work on Thursday morning.

But gradually I began to realize two important things about those young people. I realized that they were not really snobs; they were just very insecure. They were scared of each other! And I realized that they were afraid to trust me. That group had gone through four youth pastors in five years.

I determined to dig in and to do what I am convinced this generation needs from youth pastors. They need us to become men and women of God; and they need us to love them. From the very beginning of my work with teenagers I have said that youth ministry can be summed up in five words, "Love God and love teenagers." Period. I may not have a lot of talent and giftings, but I can do that.

I put a picture of each one of my teenagers into a photo album and began to pray for them by name several times a week. I asked their parents to pray with me for a move of God on the hearts of their kids.

In the spring of 1995, I was sitting at my desk one day when Holy Spirit spoke to me. It was one of those times when you know that you know that you know that God has spoken. It was just one word. "Time."

I jumped on my computer Bible program and began to cross reference the word *time*. For the next four weeks I preached to my young people about the topic. There are two Greek words for *time* in the New Testament. The first is *chronos*, which means clock, or calendar time. The second is *kairos*. This word means supernatural, divine appointments when God visits His people. In scripture it is often translated as "the fullness of time," or "at the appointed time."

The word *kairos* also has the connotation of pregnancy about it— something that is birthed in its time. At this point our church had been praying for revival for over two years; and the Sunday evening prayer meetings were getting longer and longer. What used to last from 6:00 to 7:30 would now often go from 6:00 to 11:00. We couldn't get people to go home! We were pregnant; we were expecting revival.

Every time we came to church we wondered, "Could this be the day? Could this be the day?" You could smell revival in the air like you can smell rain before it falls. You could smell it. There was such an anticipation. I remember saying, "Young people, we're fixing to experience revival!"

In our limited understanding, we thought that revival would mean a week or two of good services. We had no idea of what was about to happen.

And then came the most incredible weekend of our youth ministry. It was our *kairos* time.

We had a district youth convention in the city of Marianna, Florida, which is two hours east of us. On the Saturday night of that same weekend we were scheduled to attend a recording concert in Mobile, Alabama, which is one hour west of us. Friday afternoon we loaded up two vans with a total of 36 teenagers. We said our traditional prayer. You know, the usual, "Oh God, keep us safe, give us a good weekend, minister to us. Amen."

We weren't even out of Pensacola when one of my teens said, "Hey, guys, lets pray and worship the Lord!" Well, I learned a long time ago that when young people initiate something, I need to stay out of the way. They don't need me. I will just mess it up. I've seen this happen dozens of times so I thought, *Well, this will be cute. They'll pray and sing for 30 minutes and then start throwing spitwads.* I've been there.

To my amazement they prayed the entire two hours to Marianna. I remember pulling into the parking lot at the campground and thinking, "Dear God, I could use more of those kind of trips!" It was just wonderful. We unloaded our stuff and went to the convention. After the meeting was over about midnight we went to our dorm. We had hardly stepped through the threshold when someone again piped up and said, "Hey, guys, let's pray!"

I crawled into bed listening to them praying, while all my youth pastor friends were running through the woods trying to reign in their kids who were roaming about armed with squirt guns and shaving cream. I lay there saying, "Oh, God, You're so good to me!" My guys prayed, and they prayed up a storm. They cried and they squalled and they screamed and they sang all night long, hour after hour. The sun came up and they were still praying.

Now here is a miracle. These are teenage boys. Breakfast time came and they said, "Brother Richard, we're not hungry. We just want to pray." We're not hungry; we just want to pray?! And they prayed through breakfast. At 10:00 a.m. I made them stop praying and go to the morning service. They couldn't believe it. They were mad at me because I made them quit praying and go to that service!

When it finished around noon, we loaded up our stuff and had a couple of hours to kill. Since there is a state park right there in town, I suggested that we hang out on the trails for a little bit. Right in the middle of the intermingling trails is what I call a Florida mountain. (Anything taller than five feet in Florida is a mountain.) And on top of this mountain was a big old dead tree. I remember feeling like Moses as I got up there and sat on that stump. I watched my kids roaming up and down those trails screaming and crying out to God and praying in the spirit. It was like a light rumble of an army in the woods.

It was such a hoot to watch poor innocent park visitors. All they wanted to do was look at the birds and trees! They would come in and say, "Ooops. Wrong trail."

My kids prayed for two hours. Then I said, "Guys, we've got to get going or we'll miss the concert." So they climbed into the van and kept praying. We dropped off six kids in Pensacola, picked up six others, headed for Mobile, and they kept on praying. The concert went until after midnight. These kids had been going nonstop since Friday afternoon. It was now about 1:00 Sunday morning, and we were about halfway back from Mobile.

On Interstate 10 from Mobile to Pensacola there is about 45 minutes of ungodly nothingness. It is pitch black. There are no street lights. Lightning bugs are not even allowed to light up in this zone. It got dead quiet in the van. And that is when I turned on the dome light and saw the kids with their hands lifted and tears streaming down their face and their lips were moving quietly in the darkness.

That night I lay in bed after I got the kids home. I remember turning to my wife and saying, "Sweetheart, something big is about to happen. I'm scared to death. And I don't know what to do."

Chapter 2

A Time of Visitation

I didn't know what to do; and I was not alone. Although we had prayed earnestly and we greatly anticipated revival, Brownsville Assembly of God was not prepared when it actually happened. We did not understand that *revival* is not having a bunch of powerful services. Revival is changed attitudes, changed behaviors, and changed lives. And we did not understand how Holy Spirit intended to accomplish those changes.

I remember before revival hit, all that my pastor, John Kilpatrick, would talk about was how much he wanted a move of God. He would get up in the pulpit, Sunday after Sunday, try to preach, and then stop. "Folks," he would say, "I've just got to talk to you for a minute." He would walk around to the front, pull up the legs of his britches like he does, sit down on the platform, and begin to talk to us like daddy in the living room.

"Church, look around," he would say. "We've got a beautiful sanctuary. Things are great. Our finances are in good shape; there is no division in our congregation; we are adding new members every week.

"But church, there is more. I remember the God of my childhood. I remember the all-night prayer meetings with my pastor. I remember what it's like to wake up in the morning with a burning sensation of what was going to happen that day. I want the God of my childhood. I want revival."

It was at that point that we really started to pray. The Sunday evening service became a prayer meeting that began to last about four hours.

Our pastor became desperate for a move of God. One Sunday morning at about 2:00 a.m. he went to the church, walked through the darkness to the front of the sanctuary, and laid his keys on the altar. "God," he said, "I want to see You move. If You aren't going to send revival here, please take me to a place where You are. I don't care if it's a small congregation in the backside of the woods with 25 members. Just take me where You are going to move." He walked out and left the keys there.

Soon after that, Steve Hill, a missionary evangelist, was scheduled to do a Sunday night missions service at our church. It had been a traumatic week for Pastor Kilpatrick, and he asked Steve to preach both morning and evening. It was Father's Day, 1995, and the Father paid us a visit.

The service started at 10:00 a.m., the power of God fell, and we left around 4:00 p.m. (Actually, some people didn't leave. They were afraid that if they did, Holy Spirit would't be there when they returned.) The 6:00 evening service lasted until about 1:00 the next morning.

"Listen, folks," Brother Steve said, "I don't have anywhere to go tomorrow night. Do you all want to come back?"

Word spread throughout our community and the sanctuary was full that Monday night. The power of God fell again, and we left about 2:00 a.m.

"Listen, folks," Brother Steve said, "I have a hunch something is up. If you want, I will cancel where I was scheduled to be tomorrow and come back here." He began to cancel services one night at a time for about six or eight weeks. Then he started canceling them one week at a time. Then a month at a time. Then Steve and his family moved here. And now we are praying that God never takes His hand off this church.

When revival hit, everything else went out the window. Every program and special event was canceled. I didn't have a youth service. I didn't have a lock-in or a canoe trip, and we didn't go bowling. The only extra thing that we did do during those first three months was to attend a camp at Christ for the Nations in Texas. I love their missions emphasis, and since we had already pre-paid, we decided to go.

Talk about a trip. We had been in revival for about six weeks and my kids were on fire. We took two van loads and had CB's, supposedly to talk to each other on the road. Ha! Instead, they blasted every 18-wheeler between Florida and Texas with the gospel!

Then there were the stops at gas stations. What a hoot. You know the old scenario: "My bladder is fuller than your bladder, so get out of my way." Not anymore. When we stopped at a gas station I had never seen anything like it in my life. It looked like someone had thrown a skunk into the van. They broke windows trying to beat their friends, not to the rest room, but to the poor innocent guy at the pumps. All he wanted was a tank of gas. My kids went running to him, "Do you know God? No, I didn't ask what church you go to, I asked do you know God?"

I stayed sitting in the van; and I sat there remembering. I thought back to the last time we had taken a trip in those vans; the 33-hour prayer meeting, and how God had put a new hunger in my kids for more of Him. When the time of visitation came, they were ready. I had spoken to them about the pool of Bethesda in John chapter 5. The sick and the lame would lay beside the pool and an angel of the Lord would come and stir the waters from time to time (that's *kairos* to *kairos*). The first person to jump into the pool would be healed. I said, "Young people, listen to me. God is fixing to move; and when He moves, jump in!"

And they did! While many of us older, wiser folks were standing back scratching our heads and questioning what was happening, those young people recognized the *kairos* time of supernatural, divine visitation. They didn't care if that meant laughing, crying, or shaking. They didn't care if it meant crumpling to the floor and having to be carried out at the end of the service. They recognized God at work and jumped in.

We have been asked many times about this revival. People have criticized the manifestations and questioned the validity of what goes on in our services. To be honest with you, I myself would probably have been a critic if I hadn't been there. All I know is that God's ways are higher than ours; and I know this—when you stick your finger into a light socket, you're going to react. Any time you come into contact with power, there will be a reaction; and different people will react in different ways.

In the past, I had seen people get excited about God; but I had never seen them shake and fall to the floor until that Father's Day. I had never seen people go into trances and stay in a trance for hours, standing there like statues. Now, don't get scared. *Trance* is a scriptural word, you know. Just look at the account of what happened to Peter in Acts 10. The definition of trance according to the 1828 version of the Noah Webster dictionary is this: "an ecstasy; a state in which the soul seems to pass out of the body into celestial regions, or to be rapt into visions."

I had known and admired Steve Hill for a long time; but I had a lot of uncertainty about what was going on. Then when I saw my pastor fall to the floor, it was like, "Dear God! What is happening?"

It was only as time passed and we saw changed lives that my misgivings subsided. One example is Amy (Elizabeth) Ward. Amy was a snot. Amy was mean. Anyone who knew her, and she herself, would tell you that. Now, talk about manifestations! I saw God pick Amy up off the floor. One minute she was laying on her back, and the next she was being pulled up by an invisible force until her feet almost left the ground. Then she would drop like a rag doll. (Later Amy explained that she was holding God's hand as He picked her up; and when she dropped back on the floor, He told her that is what would happen to her life if she ever let go of His hand.) This was repeated several times, accompanied by violent shaking until about 3:00 a.m. She continued to shake for three days.

Now when you talk to Amy, she is not the same person. In fact, she felt God tell her that she needed a new name. Now she goes by her middle name, Elizabeth.

Recently I heard someone ask Elizabeth what revival means to her. Her answer made me cry. She said that it means being able to go into God's presence. It means going into her room, shutting off all the lights, sitting quietly in the darkness, and feeling God there with her. Revival means to know God and to listen to God from her heart.

As I saw fruit like this, my questions and uncertainties about manifestations didn't matter anymore. If shaking in God's presence can change the heart of a girl like Amy, I say do it, Lord! We have seen gang members, drug addicts, hookers, and church kids all get changed lives. That is all that matters to me. I don't care how God does it. If a changed life is the end result, I don't care if He shakes them or throws them through a wall!

This kind of thing is not foreign to Scripture. When people come into God's presence, things happen. The account in Daniel 10:7-10, is phenomenal:

And I Daniel alone saw the vision: for the men that were with me saw not the vision; but a great quaking fell upon them, so that they fled to hide themselves. Therefore I was left alone, and saw this great vision, and there remained no strength in me: for my comeliness was turned in me into corruption, and I retained no strength. Yet heard I the voice of His words: and when I heard the voice of His words, then was I in a deep sleep on my face, and my face toward the ground. And, behold, an hand touched me, which set me upon my knees and upon the palms of my hands.

God picked him up off the floor and set him on his hands and knees!

Look at what Job said in chapter 4, verses 14-17:

Fear came upon me, and trembling, which made all my bones to shake. Then a spirit passed before my face; and the hair of my flesh stood up: It stood still, but I could not discern the form thereof: an image was before mine eyes, there was silence, and I heard a voice saying, Shall mortal man be more than God? shall a man be more pure than his maker?

In Revelation 1:17 John fell at His feet as though he were dead. Acts 7:32 says that Moses trembled with fear and did not dare to look at God. Paul was thrown violently to the ground and God struck him blind for three days in Acts 9. Matthew 28:2-4 says,

> *And, behold, there was a great earthquake: for the angel of the Lord descended from heaven, and came and rolled back the stone from the door, and sat upon it. His countenance was like lightning, and His raiment white as snow: And for fear of Him the keepers did shake, and became as dead men.*

There are accounts like this throughout Scripture. It is just that God's people have been *abnormal* for so long that we don't know what normality is anymore. And, as I said earlier, different people respond in different ways when the power of God touches their life. Sometimes I have been praying for two people at a time. I have my right hand on one person, and my left on another. One person can be shaking and going crazy, while the other is just standing quietly.

When people go down under the power of God, we have observed how Holy Spirit has taken control, and He is speaking to them. He is speaking purpose. He is speaking hope. Many times He is just bathing them in His love and putting a yearning for Him inside their hearts. More, Lord!

I have seen young ladies laying on the floor in a fetal position, shaking and wailing. In those moments, God has healed them of painful memories of rape or other types of abuse. Many times as people are being shaken by the power of God on the outside, He is shaking things loose on the inside. He is tearing things out of them— sins they have committed, and sins that have been committed against them. He is just ripping them loose and setting them free.

Over the past months and years of this revival, I have watched the manifestations take on a quality of travailing intercessory prayer. I have watched my teenagers bow over and sometimes collapse to the floor, wailing and screaming. Sometimes it is a blood-curdling scream. There have been times when intercession like that hits the service and sinners come running to the altar, shaken to their bones. Steve Hill has said, "You think this is eerie; wait until you hear the screams from hell!" We have seen sinners collapse under conviction and have to be carried by loved ones to the altar.

Galatians 4:19 speaks about travailing in prayer until Christ is formed in people. There is something in the hearts of this generation of young people that yields to that kind of intercession, and once they have let God clean them up inside, they yield even more completely. I think it is because they understand the pain.

I know that at times when the Lord has used me in intercession, I have actually felt the pain of the person I am interceding for. This generation understands pain. They have experienced it, and that is why they are so easily used in travailing for other people's pain. They are like tools in the Master's hands— completely surrendered, completely yielded to Him.

We have seen much fruit as a result of the intercession. As Charity James, who was just 14 years old at the beginning of the revival, sings "Come running to the mercy seat..." at the altar call each evening, thousands upon thousands have literally run to give their lives to God. Many are first time commitments, and others are re-dedication to Him. Bondages have been broken, lives have been transformed, and countless Christians have received a fresh and powerful touch from God.

People ask how we can do this night after night. How can we *not* do it night after night? Fish were made to swim in water. We were made to live like this. God wants us to live and move and have our being in Him, in His presence (see Acts 17:28).

What we are experiencing is normal Christianity. Yes, we get exhausted. Yes, we get tired. There are times when we drag ourselves into the service and it takes everything inside us to get up on the platform, but when Brownsville's worship leader, Lindell Cooley hits that first note, the Spirit of God comes and nothing else matters. There is no place I would rather be.

There is a line in one of the songs Brother Lindell wrote that says, "I don't ever want to go back to my old life." A lot of Christians sing that song and it means one thing to them, but it means something different to me. They sing that song and don't want to go back to drinking or partying or the world. When I sing it, I'm singing about how I don't want to go back to "church as usual."

I don't want to go back to religion. I don't want to go back to programs. I don't want to go back to my old life. "I want to stay right here, Jesus." Right here is where I belong. This is what I was created for.

Chapter 3

In the Right Place
at the Right Time

Before the revival our youth group was about 100 strong. Now we have upwards of 700 teenagers attending each week. Of that number, I claim about 300 as "my kids." With so many out-of-town (out-of-state and out-of-country!) visitors, the only way I can know who are really mine is through our discipleship program. So, as far as I'm concerned, right now I have 300 teens in our youth group.

I have always been about discipleship, and I will always be about discipleship. One of the most common questions I am asked is how we plan to keep the kids fired up for God, how we plan to sustain the revival. The only way I know to do this is through discipleship; and I know that discipleship is on the heart of Jesus.

Listen, when a person is about to speak their final words, they want those words to count. I guarantee that they won't say, "Be sure and vacuum the living room on Saturdays." No, they choose those last words carefully.

In His Great Commission in Matthew 28, the last words that Jesus said were these: "...Go and make disciples of all nations..." (NIV). He did not say go and make believers, or go and make followers. He said, "Go and make disciples." I'm not about to try and improve on His plan.

In the midst of all my feelings when revival broke out was an intense fear. Everyone else was excited, but I was scared. I saw potential for trouble. I knew that I could end up with a bunch of shallow, emotional teenagers who were merely living off of the experience.

I can tell you right now exactly what Brother Steve will preach on tomorrow night. He's going to preach, "Sinner, get right with God! Backslider come home!" How do I know this? Because for over 600 services I have heard him say, "Sinner get right with God! Backslider, come home!" That is what God has called him to do. It is time for sinners to get right with God and for backsliders to come home! But if you are part of this church and you come to the meetings night after night after night, you can't live on "sinner get right with God and backslider come home."

I knew that my teenagers needed to become grounded in the Word. They needed to grow up. And discipleship does that. Revival will not keep them. It will not. I am not diminishing the power of the Holy Ghost, but I think it is time for us to not diminish the power of God's Word either!

I say to my young people, "When the devil comes and tempts you— and he will—what are you going to do? Will you start to shake, and expect him to run? Are you going to 'fall in the Spirit' and play dead and think the devil is going to leave you alone? No! You will have to do exactly what Jesus did! Pick up the Word of God and say, 'It is written. It is written. It is written!' "

I have used a variety of discipleship programs, and have found many of them to be "knock 'em dead" type materials: read the entire New Testament, read ten books and write a 100-page report on each one, and memorize 36 memory verses— all in 13 weeks. With programs like that, instead of making disciples, I was killing them! Now don't take me wrong, there is a time and a place for those intense programs for mature Christians. But I could never use them with these new teens off the street.

So, when revival hit, I prayed, "God! Give us a discipleship program quick— or I'm outta here!" I knew it had to be three things. Number one, it had to be simple. I'm in church six days a week! Number two, it had to accomplish what it was intended to accomplish. And number three, it had to be inspirationally good so the kids would do it!

Well, God answered prayer. He gave us the "Master's Plan Discipleship Program." It has been very successful because it is not centered around me. It is centered around Jesus, and my team of leaders. I could disappear today and people would cry for a couple of days (hopefully!) and then life would go on, and my youth group would be as strong as ever.

You see, I know that I am not some great hot shot youth pastor. I know that I do not have a lot of talent, gifts, or abilities. Because of God's love and mercy toward me, I am just in the right place at the right time. That's *kairos* time again. I know that this is my time. This is my hour. I am here "for such a time as this."

In all honesty, I am glad that I am not gifted, because I have nothing to fall back on. There are many people in the church world— speakers, musicians, artists— who are using their gifts without an anointing, and the Christian world buys their products by the millions! But I thank God that I don't have a gift to fall back on.

I live scared. This thing is bigger than me. If God doesn't show up for me, I'm in trouble. It's the truth. I love to preach, but there are a lot of preachers better than me out there. And when the Spirit of God is not on me, I am miserable in front of a crowd. My kids have seen me fall flat on my face. It's just a wake-up call. I need God.

I literally shake in my boots every day of my life now. And I have come to the conclusion that I am finally where God wants me to be. I believe that if we are not shaking in our boots because the ministry we are trying to accomplish is so big, then we are not yet doing what God wants us to do. God's ministry could never be accomplished by our human strengths and talents, only when God intervenes for us. Even Jesus began to tremble whenever He began explaining to the disciples about the crucifixion (John 12:27-28: "Now is My soul troubled..."). Whenever we begin to approach the fulfillment of our purpose in life all hell will come against us to try and scare us from glorifying our heavenly Father's name!

Youth pastor, youth leader, listen to me. When you picked up this book, maybe you were curious, maybe you were looking for some hot new ideas for working with young people, I don't know. Let me tell you right here and now—the greatest thing you can do for your teenagers is to become a man or woman of God.

Greater than having a wonderful worship team, greater than having a dynamic youth choir, greater than having a powerful drama team, greater than any of the greatest programs—the greatest thing you can do is to become a true man or woman of God. Stop chasing all the latest gimmicks and tricks for reaching teenagers. All they really want is a move of God!

This generation is hungry to see His power. Let me tell you one of my favorite stories. A few months ago three atheists—two guys and a girl in their late teens—came to our youth service. One of the guys came in on crutches. He had fallen off a car as it was driving down the highway and had badly injured his knee. (Falling off the back of a car as it is driving down the highway can hurt quite a bit.)

One of my young people had kept pestering them, and they finally agreed to come to one of our services. Throughout the meeting they made fun of what Holy Spirit was doing. That is a dangerous thing to do. At the end of the service we were praying for young people who were jerking and shaking and falling down— you know, the normal stuff. Those three teens sat and mocked.

Toward the end of the prayer time, I saw the girl running toward me squalling uncontrollably. Her face was beet red and tears were streaming down her face. "Mister! Mister! You're not going to believe what just happened!" I said, "What?" She said, "You're not going to believe it! You're not going to believe it!" I said, "What?" She said, "You're not going to believe." I said, *"What happened?"* She said, "We were over there making fun of you guys, and God healed my friend's knee!" I said, *"WHAT?!"*

Listen, I didn't know God did things like that. I thought He would strike them down, you know what I'm saying? I ran over to see this 19-year-old guy who a few minutes ago was a boastful, stuck-up kid who thought he had the world by the tail. He was sobbing like a baby, running up and down the balcony stairs. Needless to say, those three teens are no longer atheists.

This generation is longing for the power of God. Teenagers are longing for reality. Second Timothy 3:5 speaks of having a form of godliness but no power. This generation doesn't want to come to religious services. They want to come to a place where God is.

This generation wants God's power, and this generation wants to see that power as a living reality in people's lives. It is time for us to be that godly example. Listen, I may not be very gifted, but there is something I can do. I can be a good example. I can become a man of God.

With the awesome thing that God is doing in our church, it would be very easy for me to just coast along. The anointing is so powerful in every service that I could just quit preaching.

Let me tell you something. Since revival hit, I claw more carpet than ever before in my life. I am on my face before God two hours every morning. People often ask me, "What time do you have to be in the office, Brother Richard?" I don't have to be in until 9:00 a.m., but I am there most every morning at 7:30. You won't touch me for the first two hours of my morning. I crawl and scream and cry and beat the carpet for two hours. Why? Because I want to grow up and become a man of God. If I don't, God will leave me behind. God is raising up a generation, and He will do it—with or without me.

How about you, youth leader? Are you a living, godly example for your young people? In John 3:6, Jesus said that flesh gives birth to flesh and spirit gives birth to spirit. I'm going to be straight with you, my friend. The reason we have a lot of fleshly youth groups is that we have a lot of fleshly leadership. Your people are going to be just like you.

If your young people have a problem with lust, you had better check up on your own lust problem. If your young people have a problem with gossip, you had better check on your own gossip problem. Your young people are going to be just like you are. If you want to know who Richard Crisco is, come and visit my youth group sometime; you'll find out who Richard Crisco is: *We teach what we know; we reproduce who we are.*

If you get into the pulpit and preach one thing, but you are living a different lifestyle, you will have problems. Do you want to be a dynamic youth pastor? There are no shortcuts. As I stated in the first chapter, "Love God and love teenagers. Period."

So many people come to Brownsville, hoping to catch some of the fire for their own lives. They come hoping that if John Kilpatrick or Steve Hill lays hands on them it will make everything just fine. Listen to an illustration Holy Spirit gave to me to share at a pastors' conference...

I brought in a pile of firewood. On the right side of the platform I stacked up half of it like they teach the boy scouts. The rest I threw across the other side. "Pastors, listen to me," I said, pointing to the right. "Some of you are here and your home is in order. Your children are obedient; your life is in order; your church is in order. Everything is great. Everything is in place. You have come here and God is going to touch you with a coal of fire. You will take that coal to your home and to your church and they will immediately burst into flame. All Heaven is going to come down.

"But others of you, your life is in disarray. There is sin in your life. Your children are disobedient; your church, your ministry, is in a mess; and you think that if you could just get down to Pensacola, Florida, everything would be fine. There are no shortcuts in the Kingdom of God, my friend."

I spoke to those pastors, and right now, I am speaking to you, my friend. "Yes, God may touch you. Yes, God may bring a vision to you. God may do something great and you will leave this place ecstatic, but when you get home you will be frustrated because you won't see it happening. And then, after a couple weeks, you'll start wondering if God really touched you or not. And after a couple months, you might point your finger at Pensacola and say it's all just a big hoax.

"The problem is not Pensacola. The problem is you. There are no shortcuts. Get your life in order, and then God will ignite it."

Youth pastor, youth leader, I'm talking really straight to you. (In fact, I'm starting to sound a lot like Steve Hill.) It's time we started to grow up and become true leaders. I personally believe that the reason that most youth pastors go someplace for a year, and then "God" tells them to go someplace else, is that after a year they've given everything they've got. They are so shallow and immature. They go someplace else and then someplace else, yet again, and they give the same thing over and over instead of digging in and growing up.

It's time to stay put. Listen, the majority of your youth group lives in divorced homes. And many of those who have both parents at home are scared there will be a divorce in the future. They don't have stability in their schools or in most of their relationships. The only hope they have is in the church. It is our responsibility as shepherds to become secure. Before I came to Brownsville, they had gone through four youth pastors in five years! I told you in the first chapter how I used to quit every Wednesday night. Can you imagine how sick I would be today if I had left Brownsville and went somewhere else? Don't you know that I would be kicking myself!

You might be in a dry place right now. You might not be seeing things you want to see. You've been there a while, you're expecting a breakthrough, and you haven't seen it yet; you're ready to throw in the towel. Listen to me, my friend, unless God, without question, has said to move, you stay put. Very often, real breakthrough in ministry is not seen until you have been in the same place for three years.

Young people need the security of knowing you will be there. They want to know that you are going to be there for their graduation service. They want to know that you are going to be there to marry them and dedicate their babies. They need to know that you are going to be there for the long haul.

If, as you were reading, you felt Holy Spirit convict you in any areas of your life, you need to respond. You need to repent. David said in Psalm 51,

Create in me a clean heart, O God; and renew a right spirit within me. Cast me not away from Thy presence; and take not Thy holy spirit from me. Restore unto me the joy of Thy salvation; and uphold me with Thy free spirit. Then [THEN] will I teach transgressors Thy ways; and sinners shall be converted unto Thee (Psalm 51:10-13).

Right now, I want to pray for you...

Holy Spirit, I pray for this reader right now. I believe they picked up this book because they are hungry; they are tired, and they want to see You move on the young people of their church, their community, and their schools. Holy Spirit, begin to blow across their homes, across their communities; I ask You to blow away the dark clouds that hang overhead that the sun may shine on them once again. Father, anoint them with fresh vision, fresh anointing, with a fresh burden. I pray, Lord, that they would waken in the wee hours of the morning, crying and travailing over this generation. Father, let them weep for teenagers who are battered and bruised. Let them weep for this generation.

I pray, Lord, that when they stand in their pulpits, when they stand before teenagers, their words will be full of authority, full of life, full of compassion; such love that would melt the hardest of hearts. Holy Spirit, I pray that revival fires would burn in and through their lives and their ministries.

Father, let each one of us be a part of this great awakening You are bringing to America and to the world. Let us be men and women of integrity who will challenge the youth of this generation to follow hard after You.

And thank You, Lord, that in Your great mercy, You are helping each one of us to be in the right place at the right time. We want what was said of David in Acts 13:36 to be true in our lives, "...he...served God's will and purpose and counsel in his own generation" (AMP). Amen.

Chapter 4

Decision Time

The decisions you make every day influence your future and create your past. You are who you are today as a result of the decisions you have made up to this point. The quality of your decisions will directly affect the quality of your life. One of the most powerful series of teachings I have done for our young people here at Brownsville is entitled, "Decisions Determine Your Destiny."

God is looking for a generation of people with convictions. There is a big difference between having convictions and having opinions. An opinion is a preference. A conviction is something you would be willing to die for. We have a lot of opinions in the Church, but we have very few convictions. The result is Christians with little or no commitment to the purposes of God. God is looking for people who will seek Him in their decision making. He is looking for people who will seek His will and not their own.

Psalm 37:4 tells us that as we delight ourselves in the Lord, He will give us the desires of our heart. As you love Jesus with all your heart, He puts His will for you into your heart as a desire. If you are walking close to God, the things you want are the very things He wants for you!

I want to be a youth pastor. God has put that desire into my heart, and it burns within me.

Even as a child, there was a call of God on my life. I was raised in a Catholic setting and I told everyone I was going to be a priest. I believe that God had planted that desire as a seed in my heart even before I knew Him. At the age of 16, I responded to an altar call at an Assemblies of God church, and the next week I wanted to go into the ministry.

I'll never forget January 18, 1982. It was 2:00 a.m. and I had gotten home a while earlier from night school. I had completed my homework and was doing my devotions, when God came into my room.

I tell my young people to stop worrying about their future and just do what they know to do today. At 18 years of age, I was in youth choir and adult choir; I was teaching both junior and senior high schoolers at church. I had my own bus route and picked up over 50 kids every week. I did old folks ministry on weekends. I was working hard doing whatever my hand found to do. I was being faithful.

And that night, January 18, 1982, God came to me and said, "Richard, it's time." I went to my parents and they confirmed that this was the right direction for my life. The church I was attending was Milton First Assembly in Milton, Florida. I went to my pastor and he, too, confirmed that this was God's will. I tell my teenagers to seek godly counsel in decision making.

A few months later Morris Cerullo was holding a big crusade in Pensacola, about a 30-minute drive from Milton. Brother Cerullo spoke to me and said, "God has a call on your life."

That same year when I was attending Southeast Bible College, Dr. Yongi Cho was in the area speaking at a pastors' conference. The students of Southeastern were invited to attend. Dr. Cho pulled me aside and said, "God has a mighty anointing on your life. He is going to use you greatly in the future."

I didn't go seeking those words. So many people think they need to get a prophecy through some great man of God to tell them what to do. Prophecy is not to direct, but to confirm what God has already spoken to your heart.

After seminary I was faced with the major decision of where to go next. Four different churches had invited me to come and work with them. One of those churches was Milton First Assembly. The other three churches had offered me more money, but I wanted to go home and serve with the pastor I loved. Again, I sought godly counsel. I went to three of my professors, and every one of them gave me the same advice: "Richard, I believe this is God's will for your life."

Going home was one of the best things I ever did. I know the Bible says that a prophet is not honored in his own home, but I was certainly loved there. I was loved through a lot of mistakes during those early days of ministry. I was still in school, still learning.

A few years later my wife Jane and I had a beautiful baby girl, Ashley Nicole. God was about to take me to a different kind of school. I was to learn from pain and suffering. I was about to learn a new kind of decision making. Ashley was born with Hirschprung's, a rare disease. She had no nerves in her colon. For the first few months of her life, Ashley cried. She would cry all night long. She wouldn't eat. She just cried.

As parents of a first child, every one around us was giving us advice: "If you do this, or try that…"; "Don't worry, she just has colic." We began blaming ourselves for being terrible parents. We couldn't get her to sleep. We couldn't get her to eat. She wasn't gaining weight. At six months of age Ashley weighed just ten pounds.

The doctors kept running tests and more tests. Finally an old surgeon went in and did exploratory surgery and found that she had Hirschprung's disease. She had nine major surgeries, some of them eight hours long. Ashley spent one-third of her first three years in hospitals. I would go to the hospital after work and take over for Jane. We never left our baby alone; we were with her constantly.

Jane was with Ashley visiting her folks in North Carolina when the stitches from reconstructive surgery tore loose. Immediately Ashley was rushed in for emergency surgery, and I jumped on a plane to be there. One of my greatest testimonies in youth ministry happened during this time. I ended up being away from the church for six weeks that summer. When I returned the seventh week, our attendance was larger than when I left. My leaders just rallied and kept everything going while I was gone.

I remember that hospital in North Carolina. I read the entire New Testament through in a week, which is a miracle because I am a slow reader. In the wee hours one morning, I was out in the hallway reading so Ashley wouldn't be disturbed by the light. I stopped and said, "Lord, why? Why? I just can't handle any more."

The Lord spoke to me. "Richard," He said, "did I not promise that I would never put more on you than you can handle?" (See First Corinthians 10:13.) "Yes, Lord," I whispered.

He said, "Richard, I have confidence in you." In all honesty, under my breath I said, "God, I wish You didn't have such confidence in me."

He said, "Richard, I know that you will not fail me and that you will stand."

In an instant, my whole attitude toward the situation changed. Instead of a burden, it became an opportunity for me to prove my love and devotion to my loving Lord and Savior, and a chance to prove God's unfailing love and power to deliver His people. All of a sudden it was like I couldn't fail God; I couldn't let my God down. Suddenly, it was a privilege. "Thank You, Lord, that You trust me so much and You know I can handle this." Such a strength came to me. "It doesn't matter. We will make it through this. Everything is going to be fine."

Ashley got well enough to be transferred to the Sacred Heart hospital in Pensacola. I remember sometimes going right from her bedside up onto the platform to lead worship. People were blown away. "How can you do this?"

Romans 8:18 says, "For I reckon that the sufferings of this present time are not worthy to be compared to the glory that shall be revealed *within us*." Though this was one of the first verses I had ever memorized, I never understood that verse until that time in my life. I had always thought it meant that all the suffering we go through on earth doesn't compare to what will happen when we get to Heaven and see God's glory. That is not what that verse means. It means that the glory God gives to us *while we are going through the trial* is worth it.

Now when trials come my way, I say, "Thank You, God, that You have confidence in me. God, I will not let You down. I will go through this thing." As stated earlier, in John 12:23-28, Jesus said that His time of suffering had come. He was not going to ask for the thing to be removed; instead He asked for the Father to be glorified in the midst of it. That's what I want. I want my Father to receive glory as a result of my going through whatever I need to go through.

Ashley is now a healthy 11-year-old. When you look at her, you can't tell she ever had Hirschprung's. The doctors ended up sewing her large intestine side by side (instead of end to end) to her small one. That is how she has control of her bowels. Ashley is a miracle child.

Life is a series of decisions. Through every major event of our lives, Jane and I have sought godly counsel, and we have sought the Word for comfort and answers. Then, after eight and a half years at Milton First Assembly, it was decision time again.

Something had changed within me. The drive and the passion just wasn't there. For several months I struggled with confusion and restlessness. I shared my feelings with my pastor and told him that I felt God was leading me somewhere, but I didn't know where. He agreed to pray for me. "Whatever God wants, Richard. I don't want to lose you, but whatever God wants."

In retrospect, I know that I would never have left Milton on my own; God literally had to remove me. He had to kick me out of that church. I am a pastor who stays with his sheep, and if I love you, you have a friend for life. When God took His hand off of me for that church, when He lifted His anointing from my life, I was devastated. I didn't know what to do.

I sent resumés to every district of the Assemblies of God in every state in the southeast. By this time at Milton we had a youth group of 140 in a church of less than 300. I thought that was a pretty good achievement; surely somebody would want me? In six months I did not receive one phone call. Not one. I just knew that God was through with me. The feelings of confusion and despair grew so intense that I actually became suicidal. If God wasn't going to anoint me for ministry any more, then I didn't even want to live.

One day at 5:00 a.m. I called my pastor and told him I wouldn't be able to go and open the church day care that morning. It was the first time in eight a half years I had called in sick. I told my pastor that I was going to see a doctor. I didn't even have a doctor. I am never sick.

When I did manage to get an appointment, that doctor took one look at me and said, "Young man, I don't know who you are, or what you do, but you are having a nervous breakdown." He put me on medication and bed rest for a couple days.

I lay in my bed feeling like I didn't want to live. I felt like a cheap hollow tube; a cheap, hollow, good-for-nothing tube. During one of those nights I opened my Bible and began reading the story of Gideon. The Scripture says that the Spirit of the Lord came upon Gideon. In the original language, it means that the Spirit of the Lord came upon Gideon like a glove fits upon a hand.

The Lord spoke to me and said, "Richard. I have been waiting for you." I said, "Lord! I feel like a cheap hollow tube!"

God said, "Richard, I have been waiting for you to get empty of yourself and your ministry and all of the junk you have accumulated over the past few years of 'working for Me.' I have been waiting for you to become empty so I could put you on like a glove and use you once again."

This was one of the greatest wake-up calls I've ever experienced in my life. I repented quickly and was vibrant with new hope and life because I knew God was not through with me yet!

It was around that time that a friend of mine knocked at my door, and he kept checking with me nearly every day for a month. "Richard," he would say, "there is an opening for a youth pastor over at Brownsville Assembly in Pensacola. Why not give them a call?" He would contact me almost every day.

I didn't want to go to Pensacola. I wanted to leave this area of the country (I grew up here and this is all that I have ever known), and I did not want to move to a city. Compared to Milton, Pensacola is a big city. Finally I agreed to call Brownsville Assembly, provided my friend would just leave me alone. I met with Pastor John Kilpatrick and have been here for the past five years.

Did my life get any easier? No. Brownsville Assembly before revival and Brownsville Assembly since revival are two different churches. This church was very conservative, straight-laced, and proper; and so was its pastor. A wonderful place and an absolutely wonderful pastor, however, they were still conservative, straight-laced, and proper.

I've always loved to rejoice before the Lord and ding off walls, country hick style. Every song at Brownsville seemed to be in slow motion. Everything was slow, and decent, and in order. We would meet before the service and Pastor would go down the line: "At 10:00 we'll do this; at 10:05 we'll do this; I want the pulpit by such and such a time..." and so on.

The youth group consisted of 70 middle to upper class snobs. I would stand up at the youth meeting and they would be muttering, "This guy is so weird. What is his problem?" I went from a youth group who loved me to teens who ridiculed me.

I was going bananas. For two and a half years I thought I was going to die. The only things that saved me were my resolve to stay put until God called me out and my pastor's preaching. I love my pastor's preaching. He is a true shepherd who feeds his flock.

Two and a half years later, Father's Day 1995, arrived, and don't you know I'm glad I stayed. Don't you know I am so thankful to God for all He's allowed me to go through. Don't you know I am thankful.

As I look back over my life thus far, I can see strategic times of decision. And, in my work with young people, I have realized such a great need to teach them to make wise choices. Young people ask me, "Doesn't God forgive me when I make a bad decision?" And I answer, "Yes. God forgives you of your sin, but you will never forget it. He will forgive you for premarital sex, but you will still be left with venereal disease or AIDS or a child to care for." Years of destruction and heartache could be spared if teenagers would only realize the importance of their daily decisions.

How Do I Make Good Decisions?

In the series, "Decisions Determine Your Destiny," I gave my young people ten points for making good decisions. They aren't in any particular order, except that number one has to be number one.

1. *Be obedient to the things you know and understand.* As you are obedient in the daily, mundane, mediocre things in life, God will reward and expand you. See Philippians 3:12-16 and Matthew 25:21-23. So many people cry, "Lord, am I called to preach the Word? Am I called to Africa? I want to do something for You!" and they aren't even sharing the gospel with their neighbors.

Do you want to know God's will for your life? Do those things you know you should do. *Read the Word.* "I don't feel like reading" I don't either; read. *Pray.* "I don't feel like praying." I don't either; pray. *Fast.* "I don't feel like fasting." I don't either; fast. *Witness.* "I don't feel like witnessing." I don't either; witness.

2. *Go to God's Instruction Manual, the Bible.* Psalm 119:105 says, "Thy word is a lamp unto my feet and a light unto my path."

Underneath my bed is a huge box. And in that box there is a manual on everything in our house. If I am trying to assemble something, I go to the manual. If I'm trying to fix something, I go to the manual. If I want to get more usefulness out of something, I go to the manual. If your life is going haywire, or you just need direction, instead of crying and fretting, try reading the Manual.

3. *Learn from the lives of others*. This can mean both negative and positive things. I say to my young people, "How many teenagers have to die from drunk-driving accidents before you get the message? How many of your friends or your rock star heroes have to go to jail or die from an overdose before you realize that drugs will destroy your life?" I go on and on with examples.

So many young people have the concept of wanting to try things and experience things for themselves. "Brother Richard, I just have to learn the hard way. I guess I'm just stubborn." No, you aren't stubborn. You are stupid!

4. *Learn from your own mistakes*. I ask my young people, "How many of you have ever been punished or put on some kind of restriction for the same thing twice? What you need to do is look into a mirror and say, 'You can learn a lot from a dummy.' Do you want to know how to make a wise decision? Learn from your own mistakes!"

5. *Make your decisions before you are in the heat of the battle*. I compare this kind of decision making to fire drills at school. You need to understand which exit to use during an emergency. I also use the comparison of driver's

education. You need to learn how to make decisions before you get into a dangerous situation.

Many young people get into trouble sexually because they wait until they are in the back seat of some car before they ask the question, "How far is too far?" Listen, by the time you are in that back seat, your brain has shut down and your hormones are in full motion. How far is too far is a decision that must be made far in advance. I actually teach my young people that if they are even asking that question they are headed for trouble. A better question to be asking is, "How far away from that kind of situation can I stay?"

6. *Never make a decision when you are under pressure.* Most of the time when people want you to make a quick decision, it is because they don't want you to know the whole story. Do some homework before you make a decision.

7. *Consider the effects your decision will have on other people.* So many young people say, "It's my life. I'll do what I want." That is a lie. How many children of divorced parents suffer because of other people's decisions? How many parents lie awake at night worrying while their teenager "lives his own life"?

Your decisions impact those around you— especially if you are a Christian. When you receive Jesus Christ as Savior, you are no longer your own; you are part of a body. You have given up your rights. If you call yourself a Christian, act like one! One of the most embarrassing things that has ever happened to me was when I was in a school talking to the principal and some of my young people came down the hall. I said, "Oh, here are some of my young people." The principal said, "They are?" I said, "Yeah, where are they going?" "To detention."

8. *Ask God for wisdom.* James 1:5 says, "If any of you lack wisdom, let him ask of God, that giveth to all men liberally, and upbraideth not, and it shall be given him." If you need wisdom, if you need guidance and direction for your life, ask God!

9. *Ask for the mind of Christ.* Philippians 2:5 says, "Let this mind be in you which was also in Christ Jesus." I love the Christian novel *In His Steps,* in which a group of Christians asked themselves "What would Jesus do?" before every decision. I teach my young people to ask themselves what Jesus would do if He were in their situation. I tell them to pray for the mind of Christ in decision making.

10. *Seek godly counsel.* Proverbs 24:6 says, "For by wise counsel thou shalt make war: and in a multitude of counsellers there is safety."

I use the example of Solomon's son, Rehoboam, found in First Kings chapter 12. When he was faced with a major decision, Rehoboam called for the advisors of his father. King Solomon was the wisest man who ever lived, and yet he had advisors who gave him counsel. Rehoboam didn't like the advice the wise counselors gave him. Instead, he listened to what his peers had to say. As a result, the kingdom of Israel was split in two.

I ask my young people why they ask their friends for help in decision making when their friends have absolutely no idea of what they are doing either. They go to their friends because they know they will hear what they want to hear.

Decisions determine your destiny. It is time for us to love our kids enough to teach them practically, and by our example, to make good choices.

Chapter 5

Loving This Generation

*L*ove God and love teenagers. This generation is so hungry for love. Proverbs 19:22 says, "What a man desires is unfailing love." That is why many young people join gangs; that is why there is so much sexual activity. Teenagers want a sense of being loved and needed; they want to belong somewhere.

With the moral decay of society and the breakdown of families, young people are desperate for love. The vast majority of children and teenagers today do not have a father; a father who will regularly hold them in his arms and kiss them and tell them how precious they are. As shepherds, we need to hug our young people. We need to be there for them.

I know that there are lawsuits out there. In fact, to be a leader in our youth ministry you have to fill out a four-page application, get three personal references, and go down to the sheriff's office for fingerprinting and a criminal check. I take this sort of thing very seriously, but I am not going to let the perversion of this society scare me out of loving my young people.

On a regular basis, I demonstrate hugging. I ask my wife, Jane, to come onto the platform, as well as one of the young ladies. I stand directly in front of Jane, take her in my arms, and hold her real close. "This is how I hug my wife. " Then I stand *beside* the young lady, put one arm around her shoulders, and hug her that way. "This is how I hug my girls."

I hug my young ladies, and I hug my young men. For many of my young people, I am the only man in their lives who will hug them. They literally line up to get a hug. They need it. They long for it. And they long to see the demonstration of what a Christian family is.

One gal in our youth group came home in tears one night after revival. When her mother asked her why she was crying, she said, "I just saw Brother Richard and his family holding hands walking across the church parking lot, and I was just thinking about how wonderful that is."

Two teenagers whose parents were in ministry visited the revival one night. One gal's dad was a senior pastor. The other gal was from a missionary home. It was about 2:00 a.m. and I saw them slouched in their pew. I sat down, found out who they were, and said, "My children are growing up, and I don't want to make the same mistakes I have seen other pastors make. Can you talk to me for a minute?"

The tears came as soon as they began to speak. I had opened up a wound. I spent about 30 minutes with them—crying, praying, and trying to encourage them. The next night they came again; but this time they weren't slouched down in their seats. They were at the altar, and Holy Spirit was ministering to them. I hear from those girls regularly. Those girls have reinforced what has always been a heart cry of mine. I don't want to gain the whole world but lose my own family.

A common question that I am asked is how the revival has affected our home life. I am very happy to answer that revival has been the best thing that has ever happened to us. My wife, our daughter Ashley, and our eight-year-old son Caleb love this revival. They love church. They write me little notes regularly telling me that.

During the first months of the revival, however, this was not the case. We were in church every night, with the services going until the wee hours of the morning. As a church staff, we didn't adjust our schedule; we didn't even take a day off. We just kept on going. It was hard. I remember one night when Jane said, "The kids cried themselves to sleep tonight because they have not seen you in three days. You see them when they are asleep, but they haven't seen you."

It ripped my heart out. We now homeschool Ashley and Caleb. Homeschooling had been something we had previously considered doing, and the revival just helped us make that decision. I am in the office until 2:00 in the afternoon, and then you'll see my car pull out of there. I go home, spend a couple of hours with my family, take a 30-minute nap, and come back for service that night. We have prayer meeting Tuesday night; revival services, Wednesday, Friday, and Saturday nights; youth meeting Thursday night; and the Sunday morning service.

I cherish my family time. When I leave the church on Sunday afternoons, my young people know that from then until Tuesday morning, my answering machine is on. (This, by the way, is another beauty of having the ministry not built around me, but around Jesus and my team of leaders. When the teens have a problem, they don't call me, they call their leader. My phone rings less now than it did when my youth group was small!) If there is an emergency, I am available; but otherwise, Sunday afternoon and all day Monday I am my family's and my family is mine. I give them my undivided attention. They love me for it, and so do my young people. They love seeing a demonstration of a Christian family.

While we are on the subject of demonstrating loving relationships, let me just mention my relationship with my pastor. This is yet another area people ask me about. I feel that my number one job here at Brownsville is to make my pastor look good. I do whatever it takes to make that happen. In the past, I have done it all—running to the hospital, doing a prayer meeting, counseling, doing a wedding, preaching…whatever it takes to make him look good. That's my priority. I will drop whatever else I am doing, cheerfully and without complaint, and do what he has asked. And you reap what you sow! I now have more than 40 leaders whose number one priority is to make me look good!

So, as shepherds, we are to love the sheep and to demonstrate loving relationships. Another way to love them is to protect them.

When I came to Brownsville, at least 20 families told me the reason they were at our church. It wasn't because of the music or the preaching. By the way, as far as I'm concerned, our pastor *is* the greatest preacher in the world. I love hearing my pastor preach; but no one gave his preaching as the reason they joined our church. Every person told me the same thing; in fact, I wondered if they had all rehearsed it or something. They all said, "The reason we are at Brownsville is because we know our pastor will protect us."

I didn't understand that; it was so foreign to me. But now, in the five years I have been at Brownsville, I've learned what they were talking about. My pastor watches over his flock, and he will not let a wolf come in among them. He will not. The people in our congregation feel so secure. You could lead me blindfolded into one of our services, sit me down on a pew, and I could tell you whether or not my pastor is in the room. If he is not, there is a slight uneasiness. Even though other shepherds like myself are there, the people are still not quite as comfortable as with the head shepherd. When he is present, they feel safe and protected.

The very first week I was on staff, my pastor sat me down and taught me a couple things. One of those things just blew me away. "Richard," he said, "Sheep are on all fours, but the shepherd stands on two hind legs. He can see what they can't see."

My prayer since then has been, "Dear God! Help me to be a shepherd who sees what my sheep cannot see." Sheep are nearsighted; they will fall off a cliff, they are so nearsighted. As shepherds, we've got to protect them. One way to protect them is to set boundaries.

I set boundaries and guidelines for my young people, and I enforce those boundaries and guidelines. I believe that this generation has been unfairly labeled as rebellious, when actually much of what we call rebellion is merely them just screaming out for someone to tell them where the guidelines are.

Several years ago, I heard Dr. James Dobson tell an interesting story on one of his radio programs. It seems that they built some playground equipment in the middle of a large, open field. They took a class of elementary students to the field and told them that they could play wherever they wanted. For the next few hours the children stayed in the middle of the field around the playground equipment.

Then they built a big, strong fence around the field. They took the same group of children there and gave them the same instructions to play wherever they wanted to play. Within five minutes the kids were all running to the fence line. Why? Because they knew where the boundaries were. Boundaries bring freedom, not restriction.

My young people are free. They know where the boundaries are; and they know they have a youth pastor who will protect them. I will expel kids from my youth ministry. I tell my young people, "If you want to go after God, then you are in the right place. But if you want volleyball and pizza, there are a lot of churches you can go to." I expelled a guy once for doing nothing more than putting his arm around a girl in youth service.

This kid had grown up in church. I knew this kid. He had messed up several girl's lives. When revival hit, he left for a few months. When he came back, I pulled him aside and said, "I've got my eye on you. One wrong word, one cross eye, one wrong move, and you are out of here. If you want to go for God, then you are in the right place. But if you have come here to goof around, then you are out of here. Do you understand me?" "Yes sir," he responded.

A couple weeks later, there he was with his arm around that girl. I pulled him out of the service and said, "I warned you not to come here and goof off. We aren't playing games around here anymore. Go play your games elsewhere. Consider yourself expelled from this church!" He's gone, and let me tell you, my kids love me for it. They know I'm protecting them.

One night when I was preaching, six guys caught my attention. These boys had also left when revival hit, and had now returned. I am so single-minded when I'm preaching, it is pretty hard to catch my attention; but if someone does manage to do it, I get what my teens call "that look." I have this one blood vessel in my neck that pops out a mile long, my face turns red, and I look really scary.

Well, I stopped right there in the middle of my sermon, jumped down from the platform, ran to the back pew where the six boys were sitting, and gave them "that look." I stuck my finger right in their faces and said, "Listen to me, boys. If you are so determined to go to hell, you just go to hell! But let me tell you something, you are not touching anybody in this youth group; do you understand me?"

My kids went wild. They were shouting and cheering. I wheeled around and said, "And let me tell the rest of you something! If you want to go to Heaven, by all means go to Heaven. But don't you dare go alone! Take somebody with you!"

You see, when you love your teenagers, you can talk to them like that. Why do people come to this revival by the thousands to hear a man named Steve Hill screaming that they are sinners? Because Steve Hill does it with tears streaming down his face. This generation wants Steve Hill to get in their face. They want him to point his finger and say, "Young man, stop masturbating. Young lady, stop jumping into bed." They want somebody to tell them not to do those things.

But listen, youth pastor, if you don't love them and you try to do that, you had better write your resumé and get ready to move on. Rules without relationship lead to rebellion. This is so obvious between parents and teenagers. Parents say, "As long as you live in this house, you will live by my rules!" The teen says, "But Dad, I want a relationship with you." And Dad says, "I'm too busy working so I can supply all of your needs." And the teen says, "I don't need a car, Dad. I need you."

Luke 19:45 tells how Jesus went into the temple with a whip. Five verses earlier we see Jesus weeping over the city. The Lord spoke to me several years ago: "Richard," He said, "don't you ever whip the people until you have wept over the people."

I whipped those six boys that night. I sliced them open. There is a difference between a wound and a cut. A doctor has to cut you in order to remove a cancer. I don't want to wound my kids, but sometimes I have to take the surgical knife and cut them open. And it hurts. After surgery, you are going to feel badly, but it is necessary to remove that cancer.

I sliced those boys open big time. If I had just left them that way, the devil would have come and put in his poison. I *didn't* just leave them. I called each one of them the next morning, and I said, "Things have changed around here." And they each said, "Yeah, I noticed, Brother Richard." "If you want to go after God," I said, "then you are in the right place. But I'm not putting up with any garbage." And I talked to those boys. They all knew better. Since then some of those same boys have graduated from our discipleship program. You know why? Because somebody put their foot down and made it clear where the boundaries where. They love me now.

I am not about to make the same mistake I made before. When I was youth pastor at Milton, three times a week for four years I had faithfully picked up a certain young gal for church. She was a devil in a woman's suit. She single-handedly ran off at least 70 kids from our youth group during that period of time. She was constantly starting division; constantly stirring things up and running people off. But I would cry over her and I would say, "God, if I don't reach her, who will?" Well, I met her recently, and she is still not serving the Lord, and neither are 70 others.

We are the Body of Christ, are we not? And doesn't the Scripture say if your eye offends you, you should pluck it out (see Mt. 5:29)? In First Corinthians 5:5, Paul tells us to turn such a one over to satan for the destruction of the flesh; then Second Corinthians 2:10 says to accept him back after he has repented. We need to put the Scriptures into action, my friend. If you get someone in your youth ministry who is pulling other young people into sin—pulling at them to go drinking or to do drugs or to jump into bed, you need to enforce the boundaries and guidelines. And believe me, your young people will love you for protecting them. I'm not talking about blasting a kid when he falls into sin.

We all sin. I'm talking about teenagers who are playing the game and luring others into hell with them.

As shepherds to the young of the flock, we are to love and protect our sheep by setting boundaries and guidelines. We are to set a standard. We must challenge our young people to a high calling. They will live up to or down to our expectations of them. It's time to raise the standards and expectations for teens.

Chapter 6

Challenging This Generation

This so-called "Generation X" does not have a sin problem. It has a vision problem.

For over 18 years I have served the Lord in youth ministry; 13 of those years as a full-time pastor. In all of my ministry, I have not seen a generation so neglected and misunderstood as this one. Teenagers today have been abused and put down by almost every social class and organization in America. Even the Church, for the most part, has not taken the time to listen and to hear what is really going on in their hearts. Everyone is quick to jump to conclusions about the terrible mess they are in.

If this generation has major problems, it is because we have made them that way. Proverbs 22:6 tells us to train up a child in the way he should go and when he is old he will not depart from it. We have done a poor job of training.

This chapter is entitled "Challenging This Generation." Before we can do that, we must first challenge ourselves.

Isn't it amazing how we as parents or Christian leaders want to pass the blame so quickly onto our youth instead of admitting that we are responsible for their condition. That is the American way; point fingers at others instead of at ourselves. The Scriptures teach us to "confess our faults one to another" (Jas. 5:16). We will never be able to correct the problems with this generation until we first admit that *we* are the problem, not them.

I learned a long time ago that "what one generation allows, the next one enjoys."

For example, in Pentecostal arenas, just a couple generations ago, if you even went into a movie theater, it was considered to be sin. The next generation began to see "G-Rated" movies with the leery approval of their parents. That second generation then openly approved for their children to attend "G-Rated" movies and secretly allowed them to watch "PG" movies.

This third generation now has no conviction whatsoever about supporting a hellish Hollywood industry that is polluting their minds through lustful, self-gratifying scenes. They openly allow their children to watch a wide display of trash on the screen including

"R-Rated" movies. Let me remind you, I am not talking about worldly parents, I am talking about Christians!

There are many examples we could look at. Christian Americans have compromised their standards in dozens of areas for the past few decades: prayer in schools, abortion, family devotions, commitment to prayer meetings and church, and living pure and holy before God and man.

We have a standard to hold before this nation. If that standard is not held high and with strong convictions, then the children will be the ones who suffer the most.

We call ourselves Christians. *Christian* means "Christ-like." What does Christ-like mean? It means "anointed one." If you are not like the Anointed One, you have no right to call yourself a Christian. If there is no anointing on your life, don't tell anyone you are a Christian, my friend, because you will be lying. Christian means like the Anointed One.

We are supposed to be different from the world around us. Why is it that so many Christian youth ministries look, act, and sound like the world? We are no longer peculiar to the world, but rather too familiar. I get sick of reading Christian youth magazines that build youth programs around movies and secular songs. I hear youth pastors say, "Well, I've got to know what the youth are looking at; I've got to study their culture." No, you don't, my friend.

I don't have the foggiest idea what movies are out; I could not tell you the name of two rock groups. I don't have enough room in my brain to try to keep up with all the junk that's out there. I do good enough to try to learn the Scriptures. The truth is, we could never compete with the world's high-tech Hollywood industry, nor should we try.

Listen, when you talk about the latest movie, is that going to change the lives of your young people? It is not. The pure gospel is what will change their lives. I would rather have 3 kids come and listen to me preach the gospel and have their lives changed than to have 300 come to hear me give a message using the latest movie as a springboard and their lives not be changed.

If Jesus were to walk on American soil in the 1990s, you cannot tell me that He would go and check out the latest movies and rock concerts. He would give the same gospel message that He gave 2,000 years ago. "...Come out from among them, and be ye separate, saith the Lord, and touch not the unclean thing; and I will receive you" (2 Cor. 6:17).

I have been told that bank tellers do not study all the different kinds of counterfeit money so that they will be able to notice counterfeit bills. No, what they do is study and study and study the real thing, with all of its intricate details. That way they are quick to recognize anything different.

There is always going to be a new movie or a new rock group, each with its own new twist. With my puny brain, I could never keep up. Instead of studying them, I want to study the real thing. What I need to do for my young people is not relate to their culture; it is to become a man of God. My young people love my naïveté. They love my ignorance about the latest trash on the market. My young people know that their pastor is in the Word every day and that he is walking with Jesus.

In this high-tech, entertaining world, the Church has drifted away from its initial message. Too often we think that we have to compete with the world and deliver entertaining services and fancy messages. The word *entertain* appears only one time in Scripture (see Heb. 13:2) and that is in reference to entertaining angels. Please do not misunderstand me. There is a time and a place for everything; but youth ministry is about much more than entertaining teenagers.

Mario Murillo said, "You are a Christian. That means that to do anything less than what you were created to do will bore you." We have bored an entire generation by trying to entertain them. In the past two years since the revival began here in Brownsville, we have taken the youth on a total of four fellowship activities. Now I know there is a place for fun activities and that we are out of balance right now, but my kids just don't care. They would rather be in the presence of the Lord; they would rather have the power of God.

Jesus did not say, "Follow Me and I will entertain you." He said, "follow Me and you can die with Me. And when you die with Me, then you can live with Me." Reverend Leonard Ravenhill was a mentor to

Steve Hill. His epitaph says, "Is what you are living for worth Christ dying for?"

Teenagers want purpose for their lives. Every teenager who has ever lived has wanted the same thing. They want a cause to die for; and equivalent to the cause is the courage thereof. If you believe in something strong enough, you will do whatever it takes to defend that conviction.

Let me give you an illustration. I don't like Doberman Pinchers. They scare me; I don't like the looks of them. If one day I were to look out of my living room window and see a Doberman Pincher on my front lawn, I wouldn't like it. Suppose I see him prowling across the grass. His hair is standing up on his back, his teeth are bared, he is snarling, and he's fixing to set in on something. I look over in that direction and I see a stray cat. What do you think I'm going to do? I would close the blinds and say, "Good-bye, kitty. You won't walk on my car anymore." Now you cat lovers don't get angry with me; I like cats too. I'm just making a point.

Now, imagine that same Doberman, prowling across my front lawn. His hair is standing up on his back, his teeth are bared, he is snarling, and he's fixing to set in on something. I look over in that direction and this time I do not see the kitty cat; I see my eight-year-old son.

What do you think I'm going to do now? I wouldn't even take time to find a bat. I would be out of that house, taking on that dog with my bare hands. What is the difference? The difference is that there is a cause; there is a purpose. Equivalent to the cause is the courage thereof.

The reason our churches are filled with whimpy Christians is because most Christians have never caught the cause of Christ. They don't see sinners like Jesus sees them. When this generation catches the cause of Christ, they are as bold as lions. They know why Christ died. They know what they are here for. They are ignited. They catch a vision and sin has no more attraction for them; they are willing to die for the Cause.

Youth leader, it is your God-given responsibility to challenge your young people to greatness. Let me tell you a recent story about one young man who caught a vision. His name is Eric Stuberg, and he is in the tenth grade. Eric caught a vision for his school. He would come up to me and say, "Brother Richard, pray for my school! We need revival at my school. Pray for my school. Pray for my school." We prayed together almost every night.

Eric's school is about 50 miles from Brownsville, and he is in my youth group and in the revival services every night. About four months ago Eric said, "Brother Richard, we need to have a rally at my school." At this present time, we are having about two rallies at different schools every month, plus weekly campus ministries at 32 schools. I said, "Eric, you have to open the door. I can't do it. You've got to do it as a student there."

A few days later, his football coach called me. "Richard," he said, "Eric wants to have a rally here. We have tried so many Christian outreaches at our school, and they just don't work. Listen, I don't want you folks to come all the way out here, set up your equipment, and have nobody show up. We've never had more than 50 kids attend any kind of outreach like that."

I said, "Listen, Coach, let us worry about that. Trust me, if you will just put the word out that we are coming, the kids will be there." We had 350 kids at that rally. The coach was blown away: "My lands, look at all these kids!"

The first two students got up and testified. They testified about Eric. Eric had the reputation of being the blond-headed kid who carried his Bible. Each one of the teens said something like this: "One day at the beginning of the school year, I was wearing a Christian T-shirt. Eric came up to me and said, 'Johnny, listen, I'm praying for God to move here at our school, and I notice you are wearing a Christian T-shirt. But I also noticed you telling a dirty joke a while ago. I'm praying for a move of God here, and you are hindering that from happening,' he said, 'If you are not going to be a Christian, will you please stop wearing that shirt?' He wasn't being ugly or brash; he was just telling it like it is."

After those two teens told how Eric had changed their commitment to Christ, Eric stood up. For the next few minutes, he just shared his heart. "Listen, my friends. Listen to me. I don't care if you go to church; I don't care what kind of church you go to. I don't care if you wear Christian T-shirts; I don't care if you even read your Bible from time to time."

He said, "If you don't know Jesus Christ as your personal Lord and Savior, you are not going to make it to Heaven. Listen, it's more than just going to church or reading your Bible; it's knowing Jesus on a personal level."

I gave an altar call and about half of the crowd came forward for prayer. Fifty-one decision cards were turned in. The coach was blown away. The number of decision cards was greater than the number of students he had expected to attend! He came up to me with a sheet of paper with 12 names on it. "Look at this, Richard!" I said, "I know, isn't it wonderful? God is raising up a generation that is getting serious with Him."

"Richard," he said, "you don't understand what I'm talking about. I'm the football coach here. I know what I'm looking at. These 12 people are the leading football players and cheerleaders in our school. They go out partying every weekend and right now they are squalling at the altar!"

Since that rally those cheerleaders and football players have been attending the campus ministry, which is exploding out of the room they had been using. They are carrying their Bibles to school on top of their books. God is sweeping that school, and they have already called to see when we can hold another rally. "We need you to come back again."

And this is all happening because one young man caught a vision. I will say it again. This generation does not have a sin problem. It has a vision problem. Proverbs 29:18 in the King James Bible says, "Where there is no vision, the people perish." Other versions say that without vision people cast off restraints; they live carelessly.

They say a picture is worth a thousand words. One youth night I held up a ten-dollar bill. We discussed possible uses for that money. Teenagers can think of a lot of ways to use ten dollars. Then I said, "This is my money. I can do whatever I want with it." I took a match and right in front of my young people's eyes, I set fire to that ten-dollar bill.

My kids are going, "What a waste! What a stupid thing to do!" And I turned to them and I said, "That *was* a stupid thing to do, but not nearly as stupid as what some of you are doing with your lives. Your life has great potential. Your life has usefulness. God has a plan and a vision for what He wants you to accomplish. Are you going to foolishly waste your life or are you going to give it to Him so He can make it count for something of eternal value?" My kids got the picture.

The greatest deterrent to sin is not rules and regulations; it is vision. You can preach hell hot and sin black as long as you want to, and it may do some good for a little while, but it won't stick. I appreciate what President Reagan tried to do for America's drug problem with the "Just Say No" campaign, but there is fallacy in that program. You can't say no until there is a bigger yes to say yes to.

Take Junior High Johnny for example. He is all slouchy with his shirt hanging out, his shoes untied, and his hair messed up. Every morning his momma says, "Johnny, brush your teeth. Johnny, comb your hair, tuck in your shirt, and tie your shoes. Please, Johnny, you're embarrassing me!" Five minutes out the door, Johnny looks like a slob again. This happens every morning.

But then one day at school, Johnny notices Suzy for the first time. He looks across the classroom, and Suzy winks at him. All of a sudden, miracles begin to take place. The boy's combing his hair. He's tucking his shirt in. He is bringing his toothbrush to school to brush his teeth! And his momma goes, "Hallelujah! I knew if I kept nagging him long enough, he would hear me!"

He never heard his momma. He caught a vision.

When God comes down and visits a young person, and He opens his or her eyes to the call of God that is upon his/her life, all of a sudden, that young person will become consumed with that vision. All of a sudden the things of the world have no more attraction. That person will say, "I don't want to drink; I don't want to jump into bed; I don't want to get high. I want Jesus! I want to do what He has called me to do!"

For some reason, we have thought that if we were ever to challenge our young people, if we were to put demands on them, they would leave. Listen, schools don't mind making demands on our young people. Football teams and cheerleading squads and bands don't mind putting demands upon young people. Why? Just so they can march out in front of a crowd for a few minutes and do their thing.

Young people are looking for purpose. They are looking for a cause to die for. It is our responsibility to create vision and a cause within our young people; to challenge them to rise up and be who God created them to be.

David was a man after God's own heart. In Acts 13:22 in the Amplified Version God says, "...I have found David son of Jesse a man after My own heart, who will do all My will and carry out My program fully." Acts 13:36 tells us that David fulfilled God's purpose in his generation.

This is the challenge to set before your young people: that they too will fulfill God's purpose, will, and vision for their lives in this generation.

Chapter 7

Setting the Standard

STOP DATING!

That is what I tell my young people. And they love me for it.

One night I brought a big white board to our youth meeting. On one side I wrote "Positives: physically, spiritually, emotionally, and socially." On the other side I wrote "Negatives: physically, spiritually, emotionally, and socially."

I said, "Tonight we are starting a new series on dating versus courtship. I want you to preach to me tonight. I want you to talk to me. First, give me all the positive things you can think of about the American dating system. List them under one of those four categories."

You should have seen their eyes. They spent the next ten minutes struggling to come up with positive things to list. My kids are so ingenious though. They even came up with something positive to list under the physical category. Do you know what it was? "It promotes good health and hygiene." Very good. Do you want to date? Stay in shape. Good.

I asked them to now give me the negative things and put them in the categories. For over an hour, I wrote as fast as I could write. When my hand started to go into spasms I said, "Listen, it's 9:30 and some of you have tests tomorrow. Let me stop." There were still 40 hands in the air. I said, "Before you go home, I want to ask you one question: Can you honestly look at this board containing your list and with any integrity tell me that this is the will of God for your life? I don't think so."

I'll never forget the next week either. I said, "God is looking for a generation that will stop chasing after britches and skirts and go after Jesus! Stop dating! Go after God!" They erupted in applause. Then I said, "Listen, we are out of time. I've got to shut up. We'll come back next week."

Well, you would have thought we were at a Carmen concert. They stood up in unison and started chanting, "More, more, more, more!" And I thought, "Dear God! I'm telling them to stop dating, and they're going bananas!"

For the first two weeks of that series, which is entitled "A Match Made in Heaven," I just showed my kids the fallacies of the American dating system. After the second week, one of my young ladies came up to me and said, "Brother Richard, today a guy at work asked me out on a date. I told him that I don't date. I court."

I asked what his response was and she told me that he walked away. I said, "This is only the second week of the series! You don't even know what courting is yet, do you?"

"No," she replied, "but I do it."

This is where this generation is at. They are ready for a higher standard. They are ready for the Book. They don't want what the American dating system is giving to them; they want what the Bible has to say.

I personally believe that the American dating system is a lie from the pit of hell. I don't believe it sets people up for marriage; it sets them up for divorce. If dating is good preparation for marriage, why does America have the highest divorce rate in the world?

The old song says, "Breaking up is hard to do," but the more you do it, the easier it becomes. Dating is preparation for divorce. People get so used to breaking up that breaking up a marriage comes easily.

The Christian community has taught our young people, "Save your body for one person. Save your body for your husband or wife." Then we turn around and say, "But go ahead and give your emotions to a lot of people. Go ahead and give your heart away to as many people as you can."

My young people love the protection that courtship gives them. The guys aren't feeling pressured to ask girls out. My girls don't have to go on a date with some jerk face just because they are too embarrassed to tell him no. Let Dad do it! My girls love it.

Dating destroys the strength of your youth ministry. You know that, don't you? A guy and a girl who love Jesus with all their hearts...they get together, and the whole church is excited about the new couple. The next thing you know, both of them are not on fire for God, and they are struggling with sexual issues so they split up because they don't want to fall into sin. They split up, and pretty soon the guy starts dating another girl and now you have division and jealousy in your youth group. I've seen it for years.

Since our standard of courtship was introduced, I have very little of that kind of thing going on. There are guys and gals in our youth group who are best friends, and there is not a romantic extension in it. They are relieved of that pressure because they know they are not going to the next step. They are just so free to enjoy each other's friendship.

Their commitment is also making a great impact on others. For example, a youth group from Virginia visited Brownsville recently. They attended the Thursday night youth meeting and then they came to the Friday night revival service. That night has become one of our "historical" services. The power of intercession began to slip over the congregation. People were moaning and groaning by the hundreds in repentance before the Lord.

That youth group sat through both services basically unmoved and unchanged. On Saturday my assistant youth pastor, Donnie Lewis, invited them, as well as some of our young people, to his home. This youth group began to talk to our kids, and all they kept asking them was, "Who are you going out with? Who are you interested in? Who are you dating?"

Every one of our kids said, "I'm not dating anybody. I'm not interested in anybody. We're all going after Jesus."

This is what happened. Holy Spirit convicted their hearts right there at Donnie's. God radically got hold of them and transformed their lives that day. The service Thursday night didn't do it; the service Friday night didn't do it. But when they heard about a group of young people who were chasing after the Lord instead of the opposite gender, it broke their hearts.

In First Corinthians 7:32-38, Paul tells how unmarried men and women are concerned about pleasing the Lord, while those who are married are concerned about pleasing their spouses. Single people can go after God with all of their hearts. Married people have divided affections. In verse 35, Paul explains that he is saying this for "your own good, not to restrict you, but showing you how to live in a right way with undivided devotion to the Lord." Paul is saying that he wants us to be free from anxiety and concern.

I feel that one of satan's major attacks against this generation is through this dating thing. This is the only time in their lives they can serve God without any distractions. The devil wants to get them sidetracked by chasing after britches and skirts.

Well, when I introduced this teaching, the only problem I encountered was the parents. The kids were ready, but their parents were not. Here is one illustration I use to help parents understand.

Fathers, suppose you just got a brand spanking new car, the BMW or whatever vehicle you've always dreamed of owning. It is parked in your driveway. Now suppose one evening a young good looking fellow who is about 18 years old comes knocking on your door.

You open the door and he says, "That sure is a sharp-looking car you have there in your driveway. You mind if I take it for a spin? I just want to go down to the restaurant for a while, and maybe over to the movie theater. I'll bring it back in a couple hours."

Dad, you would say, "Who in the world do you think you are? Who in the world do you think you are?!" It wouldn't matter how good looking or how straight-laced he seemed to be. You are not about to give the keys of that car to some kid you don't know.

Yet, a young fellow who you don't know can come knocking at your door—that is, if you're lucky he will come to your door; he may just sit in the car and beep the horn— and he wants to take your daughter out for a couple hours, and off they go! You don't know this guy from Adam. I don't care what he looks like. Perverts come in all shapes and sizes. Some of the best-looking guys are the ones you had better watch out for.

Think about it, Dad.

Next to giving their lives to Jesus, the most important decision young people make is who they will spend their future with. I believe that God wants young people to honor their parents by allowing them to give direction to their social lives. Our definition of courtship is this: "Courting is a father's agreeing to work with a qualified young man to win his daughter for marriage."

Whenever I share this teaching with youth pastors, a barrage of questions follows. You will probably have several of your own. If you want more information on dating versus courtship, the audio cassette tape series, "Match Made in Heaven" is available.

In the courtship process the single person remains focused on pursuing the Lord and is not distracted by trying to find a mate. This is basically what is referred to by Proverbs 18:22 which says, "Whoso findeth a wife findeth a good thing...." Let me illustrate what this verse means in it's original language. Have you ever been walking down the street and happen to see a quarter on the side of the road. What do you do? You stop, pick up the quarter, and keep walking toward your destination. Were you looking for the quarter? Was that the reason you were walking in that direction? No. You were on your way toward a specific destination, minding your own business, and you just happened to find the quarter lying there. This is what this Scripture is alluding to. A man is going after God with all of his heart and while he is in pursuit of the Lord, he stumbles upon his wife, picks her up, and continues to follow the Lord. He is not searching for his wife, but for the Lord!

In the courtship process, the decision to marry is based on God's will, and confirmed by parents and others in authority rather than emotional or hormonal impulses. The period of courtship is for the emotions to catch up with the prayerful and rational decision. Our emotions are not to lead us but to follow us.

Christians are always talking about walking by faith and not by feelings; but when it comes to our mate selection, we walk almost entirely by feelings. In America we say, "Marry the one you love." The Bible says, "Love the one you marry."

In closing this chapter, let me clarify that I by no means believe that all of my youth are committed to courtship, but I do have about 150 who have signed covenants with their parents surrendering their romantic lives to their authority. It has made a drastic improvement in our ministry.

It is God's plan. Let's lift the standard and watch our young people rally to it.

Chapter 8

Master's Plan Discipleship

John 1:12! Romans 3:10! 3:23! 5:8! 6:23! 10:9 and 10! First John 1:9! Come on, youth pastor! Come on Christian leader! Let me hear you quote these verses!

Sadly, many of you can't do it. You don't even have the plan of salvation verses hidden in your heart. No wonder you don't witness. No wonder you are so cowardly. You aren't equipped for the real work of the ministry.

My kids in Master's Plan Discipleship can quote those verses. Right now many of them can say over 40 Scriptures. They are equipped; they know what they are talking about. Why? Because they memorize a verse every week. Line upon line; precept upon precept; here a little, there a little. That's all it is, my friend. Discipleship is not just a program. Discipleship is a lifestyle.

As a shepherd to my young people, one of my responsibilities is to feed them. I believe that I need to do my very best. Just as my pastor does his best to feed the congregation Sunday morning, I need to do my best to feed my young people Thursday nights. Youth are not second-class Christians. I do my best to gorge them with the Word so they have something to chew on all week long. You will not touch me on Thursdays. I spend the whole day preparing to feed my kids. I want them to be strong and healthy.

I prepare four pages of notes including my outline, Scripture references, and places for them to write while I preach. These pages are folded over with holes punched for them to put right into their discipleship notebooks. The majority of my discipleship students carry their notebooks and their Bibles to school, right on top of their other books.

And they re-preach my sermons at their campus ministry meetings. They re-preach my sermons to kids in the halls, in the bathrooms, and in the cafeteria. Maybe they meet someone who is depressed and suicidal. They say,"Wait. Three months ago Brother Richard talked about that...wait a minute...here it is...." And they share with that young person; they have a word; they are ready to give an answer. It's beautiful.

I am seeing God raise up powerful, powerful young people. The kids in our discipleship program are my heroes. I tell them that regularly. They really are my heroes. I am so proud of them; I am so impressed by their boldness and zeal for God.

At almost every youth meeting, I pull five or six kids up onto the platform and say, "These are some of my heroes. These kids live for God every day. They are praying. They are reading and memorizing the Word. They are witnessing." Then I turn to the kids on the stage and say, "You really are my heroes. I love you guys." I hug them and I usually give them some kind of gift, a T-shirt or CD for example. By doing this, I am publicly acknowledging them, and I am also provoking the other teens to get into Master's Plan. They wish they were up there on that platform getting that gift.

During the first term of Master's Plan Discipleship I had the privilege of being the coordinator for Carmen's tour in this area. Carmen gives a jacket to all of his coordinators. My kids *loved* that jacket. I held it up in my youth meeting and I said, "I'm going to give this jacket away in a few weeks; but if you are not in discipleship, sorry. You don't qualify." And all the kids out there were kicking themselves and saying, "Why didn't I get into discipleship? Why didn't I get into discipleship?" Hebrews 10:24 says, "And let us consider one another to provoke unto love and to good works." I do all I can to provoke, to stir up, and to stimulate my young people to discipleship.

Master's Plan is so simple. My 8-year old son and 11-year old daughter can do it. I ask my young people to read three chapters every day. They read an Old Testament chapter, a New Testament chapter, and a chapter from Proverbs; they read through Proverbs 12 times a year. Each week for ten weeks they memorize a Scripture. In order to graduate, one of the requirements is to write out those Scriptures. If they are in the second, third, or fourth level, they also have to write out the previous verses.

Other requirements to graduate are taking sermon notes and keeping a personal journal. (I wish someone would have told me to keep a journal a long time ago!) They are expected to witness at least once a week.

Proverbs 11:30 says, "he that winneth souls is wise." Acts 1:8 says, "...ye shall be witnesses unto Me...." I teach my kids there is a difference between winning souls and witnessing. Most people are not gifted soul winners; but every one of us is called to be a witness. In a court of law a witness gives an account; he merely tells what he has seen and heard.

It is not the job of the witness to convince the judge to make a certain decision. That is the job of the lawyer. It is not our job to pull people's hair and twist their arms until they accept Jesus. Holy Spirit is the One who convicts them of their sin; it is His responsibility to draw them to Jesus, not ours.

Teaching this to your teenagers will liberate them. My kids know that no matter what results they see, they have been successful. The person they talk to about Jesus might spit in their face and swear; or he might fall to his knees in repentance. Either way, my young people have done their part. They have opened their mouths and given a witness of what they have seen and heard.

My kids are so free. They understand their role, and they know the Word. They are as bold as lions. In fact, they scare the living daylights out of me. Every Friday night they blitz the neighborhoods around our church. These streets are the worst streets in Pensacola. These streets have been known for years for prostitution, drug dealing, and gangs.

At the schools, a literal war is going on. My kids get hate mail. They get threatening letters from satanists at school all the time. They bring these letters to me, and are they scared? No! In fact, they are literally glowing because they are so excited. "Look, Brother Richard! It says 'I hate you. You will be dead next week.' Isn't that great, Brother Richard?! I just know God is going to move at my school!"

All of this stems out of discipleship. I've asked the Lord why my kids are like this and He shared with me, "They are in the Word. They know what they are talking about. Secondly, they are spending so much time in My presence that they have caught My heart for the lost. They are in revival services several times a week. Number three, they are clean." (How can we tell somebody they are living in sin if we are living there ourselves?)

The Lord said, "Number four, they spur one another on." My kids go out in groups, and they have added boldness. How many times have you done something with some of your friends that you would never had done alone? They wait in the parking lots of nearby convenience stores, and I'm not kidding you, they stalk their prey. Some poor guy pulls up. All he wants is a coke and a Snickers bar. And they wait for him.

"He's in the aisle...He's at the cash register...Here he comes." The guy opens the door to his car and three teenagers jump on him. "Hey, do you know Jesus?" I'm trying to train them to use a little tact, but hey, I would rather have them like this, than have me try to motivate a pack of dead teenagers!

It all starts with discipleship; and the key is through leadership. Youth pastor, leadership is the key. Jesus discipled 12; how do you expect to handle 20? You can't do it. I have almost 50 leaders. Most of them are about college age. About 15 of them are older adults.

Let me tell you something here. When most youth groups get really big, they are split into junior high, senior high, and college age. If that works for them, fine; but I don't do that.

One reason I keep them all together is because I don't like the attitude that senior highers develop toward the junior highers. They look at them as the little church kids. I will not put up with that.

As I said in a previous chapter, when I first came to Brownsville, the youth were known as the snobs of West Florida. To combat that attitude, I did two different series of teaching. I like to teach in four week series because teenagers don't get it the first few times they hear a message. (And don't fool yourself, they don't hear you either!) I say the same thing in different ways over and over until it gets through to them. I preach something until they are preaching it with me.

One series was entitled, "Haven of Rest" and the other was "City of Refuge." I told the young people, "This place is going to be known as a place where it doesn't matter how you look, how you dress, how you talk, or how you smell. This is going to be known as a place you can go and be loved and accepted."

I train my young people that close friendships are good, Jesus had special friends, but I never want their cliques to get so tight they won't reach out to someone else. I teach them to greet two or three people they don't know before they go and talk to their friends. If you ever visit one of our youth services, I guarantee you will shake several hands before you even sit down. You will feel welcome.

So, when I came to Brownsville, I taught the kids to reach out. I started taking high school students aside and I said, "Listen, I know you want to do something for God, right? Listen, Jeff, I have an incredible ministry opportunity for you right now. You can do something for God right now that would really impact a life. Do you see that junior high kid over there? Josh is his name? Well, I've noticed that Josh always sits off in that corner by himself. And I've also noticed him watching you. Remember when you were in junior high school how you looked up to the high school students and thought that they were so cool. Remember how you used to admire them. He looks up to you. You could really make an impact in Josh's life. Would you befriend him, and see if he will start sitting beside you?"

I develop an attitude in them of looking at the junior highers as opportunities for ministry. And when my senior highers graduate, I take them out for a coke and I say, "You are no longer a high school kid. If you want to continue to come to youth ministry, you are welcome to do so, with this understanding: You are no longer coming to be ministered to, you come to minister. You will start coming to my leadership classes and you are going to move into areas of ministry." This is where my greatest number of leaders come from.

Leadership meetings are every Sunday morning before the service for one hour. During that meeting we go through the next week's discipleship lesson that they will be doing with their kids. They stay one week ahead. I get them to tell me what they learned from that week's chapters. I get them talking. If a key point has gone unnoticed, I bring it to their attention and ask them to make sure their kids pick up on that particular principle.

Each group has six kids—guys with guys and girls with girls. There is one leader plus a leader in training. Usually in each group there is a college student who wants to be a leader. In order to do that, he or she must first go through the program. The next term, that college student comes alongside the leader and works with them, and in that blank space, I will put another college student. The next term, we give that person their own group. That is how we multiply; new students go to the new leaders.

The leaders meet with their group of young people in a room here at the church for one hour before their choice of one of the evening services. They pray, quote their memory verses, and discuss the Scriptures they had read that week, this time with the leaders getting the kids to talk. They don't sit there and preach at them. This program is not just cramming the kids full of information; it is teaching them to hear from God for themselves. My leaders come up to me every week and say, "Brother Richard, you would not believe what my kids just taught me! And we ran out of time again."

In addition to the weekly meetings, the leaders phone each of their kids and mail them a letter every week. Teenagers love to get mail. I supply the letter-head paper, envelopes, and stamps. I am real big on writing notes. I try to write three thank you notes every day. I believe in appreciating and honoring people.

I learned from John Maxwell that my level of success will be determined by those who are closest to me. I am successful because those around me want me to be successful. There is no way I can do what I am doing alone. Leadership is the key. I pour my life into my leaders every Sunday morning.

I am constantly reading books, and every time I find a good one, I buy dozens of copies and pass them out. I pour my life into my leaders, and I ask them to turn around and pour their lives into six teenagers.

Our Master's Plan theme verse is First Thessalonians 2:8, and I'm paraphrasing, "I love you so much that I gave to you not only the gospel, but also my very soul." Listen, my friend, anyone can get into the pulpit and preach. In the atmosphere here at Brownsville, the excitement level is so high, the presence of God is so strong, someone could get up there and sneeze and there would still be people who would race to the altar. Anybody can get up and preach, but it takes somebody special to pour their life into another.

I tell my leaders, "If you will love your young people, they will follow you to the moon. Pour your life into them and they will follow you anywhere. This program rises or falls upon you. The materials are great, but it's going to take you putting your heart into it for it to be effective."

Let me tell you something wonderful. At the end of every discipleship term, the kids fill out a form. One of the questions I ask is whether they would like to switch to a different leader next term. We are now finishing our fourth term. In all this time, not one person has asked for a different leader. Every one of them has said, "I love my leader. He (or she) loves me. I want to stay with them." That is a miracle. My leaders are doing their job.

People ask me about my long-term goals. Here is my 15-year goal: If you go up to one of my kids 15 years from now and ask them, "Why are you serving the Lord today?" I want that person to respond, "Fifteen years ago I was part of one of the most dynamic youth ministries in the world. I had the greatest youth pastor in the whole world." (I teach them to say that. They even bought me a T-shirt that says that. I wear it for them, because I know that I will rise to their level of expectations for me.)

"But the reason I am serving the Lord today is because of my discipleship leader. There was a young lady named Brandy who took me underneath her wing and she loved me. She cried with me; she prayed with me; she went to my ball games, she was there when I needed her. Brandy was my hero. I wanted to grow up and be just like Brandy."

At the end of each term we take a three-week break to re-enlist and sign up new students. Ninety percent re-enlist. They love discipleship. We are presently nearly finished our fourth term, and I am writing the materials for the fifth. We will just keep on going. I will write one term ahead of where they are. We plan to have a glass display case erected in the church foyer. The young people's names will be put on name plates and moved from level to level to level as they graduate. It will serve both to recognize them and to challenge them to go on to the next level.

At our last Master's Plan graduation, I honored all of the leaders at the Thursday night youth meeting. Then those leaders gave the graduation certificates out to their kids. As they called out their names, they each came forward. Time after time after time, the young people would hug their leader and cry and then grab the mike and say, "I have the best leader. He prays for me; he cares about me. I have the best leader." Then the next young person would come up and say, "No, I have the best leader." And they were all bragging on their leaders.

I was sitting off to the side of the platform in my chair. Out of 197 students who graduated that night, not one of them said, "I love Brother Richard." Not one. And I was sitting there, proud as a peacock. I felt like a proud papa. I don't need their praise and accolades. If everything is centered around me, it is not centered in the right direction.

I was so excited. I am still so excited. My 15-year goal is already being accomplished.

I have had another goal burning in my heart for many years. One of the most painful things for me about youth ministry is to birth a vision in a young person to do something great for God and then send them off somewhere else to be trained. I am not against Bible colleges; I myself am a product of Southeastern Bible College. I have sent dozens of kids there, but it has been painful for me. I wanted to be part of their training process.

For the past number of years I have spoken to Pastor Kilpatrick and the other staff members. I even drew up a plan. I tell you, this has been burning inside me, especially recently. I don't want to send my kids away from this revival.

Well, in the fullness of time, that vision has come to pass. I am now one of the professors at Brownsville School of Ministry. It is a two-year, very intense program. At the end of two years, students can graduate as a licensed preacher with the Assemblies of God.

When Dr. Michael Brown came to Brownsville, God spoke to his heart about starting the school, and it was birthed in two months. In our first term we had 120 students. I don't have to run it, I am just a professor; and I get to teach my two favorite subjects: Youth Ministry and Discipleship! God is GOOD!

As an aside here, when it is *kairos* time for something, as I wrote about back in the first chapter, it is amazing how God puts people in place to make it happen. When revival hit, every program we had went out the window. Many of them were so dead, all we had been doing was struggling to keep them alive anyway. Now we begin things only as someone gets the vision for it.

My worship leader, Mike, came to me at the beginning of the revival and said, "I'm going to be part of the worship team." Mike didn't even know what a keyboard was. Two months later he was playing one and leading worship. His anointed ministry was birthed by God. That is the only kind of ministry I want.

I would love to have a drama ministry, but I don't. Often youth pastors ask me about our drama ministry. It would be so great to have a team minister at the school rallies with us. I neither have the time nor the talent to begin a drama ministry. I could appoint one of my leaders to do it, but I won't do that. Instead, I will wait, and pray. *Kairos* time will come. The right person will come along. They will be gifted and they will have the burden. And the ministry will be God-birthed and anointed. It won't be some lifeless thing that I have to keep trying to pump up.

Just recently the Lord sent us two gifted musicians, Bill and Lisa Ancira. They have helped us develop a powerful youth choir with 150 voices. When the youth choir sings the church goes wild with praise and excitement. It was *kairos* time for our choir.

Back to discipleship—John Maxwell says, "There is no success without a successor." My responsibility is to motivate my young people, and now my students, to do things that I will never do. I am to lay the groundwork for them. David was a great man of God, but he didn't get to build the temple; his son Solomon did. But David had collected all of the materials and gotten all the workers in place. He made it possible for Solomon to succeed and exceed him.

Another of my life's dreams, which I realize now that I personally won't fulfill, was to go to the mission field. I love missions, and I impart that love to my kids. A young man named Joey Gordon was birthed out of my youth ministry. He is now in India, touching thousands of people. I see Joey doing things that I will never do, and that's my job.

Youth pastor, your job is to challenge your young people to excel you. You are to lay a groundwork and challenge them to do great things for God. This generation is looking for a purpose and a cause to die for.

Let's give them the Master's plan for their lives.

Chapter 9

Shaking Our Community

God's heart is for people. His heart is for the lost. This move of God must not be contained within the walls of a church building. This revival must affect our communities; it must cause us to infiltrate society. When God touches you and revives you, it is not just for you to feel good, my friend. It is for a purpose.

Brownsville Assembly of God is attracting visitors from all over the world. I never want our ministry to youth to bring any kind of reproach to my Savior. When visitors come, I want them to see young people who are on fire for God and as solid as a rock. I want them to see teenagers who are changing their world for Jesus. And I am telling you, as youth pastor of Brownsville Assembly, I've got the greatest group of young people I've ever met in my life. My kids are true blue to the core. They aren't just getting revived, they are carrying the message of Jesus everywhere they go.

I have a newspaper clip hanging in my office from a recent Pensacola News Journal. It says how our county, Escambia County, "bucks the system." It says that statewide, juvenile crime rose 1% last year, but in Escambia County, it dropped 13%! Now that is meaningful to me.

At the end of the summer in 1995 I told my young people, "I have watched you shake and tremble and cry for the past three months. Now I want to see you shake your schools. God has touched you; now I want to see you touch the world."

In the next few months we went from being involved with 3 campus ministries to over 30, at an average of 3 new ministries each week. We are now part of a campus ministry in every college, university, junior college, high school, and junior high school in this area. And I'm not talking some wimpy three-or-four-persons-in-a-group stuff; some of our ministries now meet in gymnasiums because there are no rooms large enough to hold them.

These campus ministries are student initiated and student led. In my past 12 years of experience in this area, I have observed how the kids often start off strong at the beginning of the year, then fade. They have usually lacked both leadership and materials. I now meet with the campus leaders as a group once a month to challenge them and to let them encourage each other.

I am constantly buying books and putting materials into their hands. I have given hundreds of dollars worth of materials to students who don't even attend our youth group. For example, we have Baptist students who lead a campus ministry at their school. We invite them to come to our monthly leadership meetings to receive support and materials.

I teach those leaders how to gain added favor in their schools. I tell them to find out all of the teacher's birthdays and to send them birthday cards. I encourage them to volunteer to serve, to clean the teacher's blackboards, etc. "Jesus said He came to serve; follow His example. Serve your school!"

When I first came to Escambia County, I went around and introduced myself to all the principals. Over and over their response was to throw their hands in my face and tell me to stay away. You see, other youth pastors in this area had done some stupid things. You know what I mean, they had overstepped the boundaries that had been set for them.

Well, for the next two years I tried to keep my nose clean and just watched for opportunities to serve and to gain favor. Soon after the revival started, a number of the principals started to call me up and ask me out for lunch. I couldn't believe it. They would ask me if I wanted to start a campus ministry or if I would like to come to their schools and eat lunch with the kids.

One of the principals took me aside and explained this change in behavior. "Richard," he said, "every month the principals and school boards get together and discuss education here in the county. Well, at our last meeting, during the break time, some of the principals were talking and the topic of your revival came up and we decided that we needed to take advantage of what is happening at your church."

God has given us such favor. I even have a couple plaques on my office wall from schools thanking me for adopting them as partners in education.

If there are ever complaints about what goes on in our campus ministries or at the rallies we hold at schools, I always take the heat. I always protect the principals. I never say things like, "But he said we could do it. We had his permission." No, I take the heat and I do all I can to make the principals look good. I do all I can to gain their trust and respect. Always remember, the principals can be your best friends or worst enemies. I want them as friends.

Recently I met with the superintendent of schools in this area. I was planning to have kids blitz his schools with 6,000 pieces of literature about the "True Love Waits" campaign, and I wanted him to see the materials in advance. I didn't need to do that, because young people have the right to distribute literature on campus, but I feel it is important that he is never caught off guard.

I began the meeting by saying, "Here is what we are planning to blitz your schools with. I want you to know that I am here to serve you, and I never want you to be embarrassed because you weren't informed...."

Right in the middle of my sentence that superintendent said, "Stop right there, Richard. I want to tell you something. I had to leave a school board meeting to come to this meeting with you. It was running late, and when I excused myself I explained that I had an appointment to meet with Richard Crisco.

"Their ears perked up and they said, 'Oh, what does he want?' I said, 'He wants to do the True Love Waits campaign at our schools.' They asked me, 'Well, what are you going to do?'

"And I answered, 'I will let Richard Crisco do anything that he wants to do because I know I can trust him.' "

Talk about favor! I do everything possible to gain this kind of attitude, but there *are* things that happen which simply are beyond our control. Take shaking for instance.

The first school year of the revival, I received a lot of phone calls about kids shaking at school. Every school would handle it differently. Some schools take those students to the back of the room; other schools put them in a different room; and other schools put them right out of the school! We have had kids get suspended for shaking.

I remember one call I got from a local principal. She said, "Is this Mr. Crisco?" I said, "Yes, Ma'am it is." "Are you the youth pastor at *that* church?" "Yes, Ma'am, I am." She said, "I need your help." I said, "I will be glad to help you in any way that I can."

She said, "I have 12 students shaking violently in the hallway. Can you come here?" "Yes, Ma'am. I'll be right there."

I hopped in my car, thinking, "They didn't teach me this stuff in Bible College." I got to the school, and there was the principal with about half a dozen teachers behind her, all standing with their arms crossed. They didn't speak but I could feel them asking me, "Okay, weird man of God. What is going on here?"

I cleared my throat. "Before I say anything, may I see the kids?" They took me to the classroom where the students were shaking. I didn't know any one of them. I thought, *Holy Spirit, if You are going to do this, at least give me some leverage, you know?*

I turned to the principal and asked why she had called me. She told me the only thing they could get out of them was the name of our church. I thought, *Help me, Lord.* I said, "Okay, listen. This is a junior high public school. You know that junior highers are the cruelest people on the earth. They eat their young. The last thing these kids want is to be different. They don't want to be made fun of. They don't want to be isolated."

The principal nodded, and I continued. "Do you honestly think that on their own initiative these kids are going to shake and look like they're having an epileptic fit in the middle of changing classrooms, in front of their classmates, knowing they would be ridiculed and made fun of?"

And believe me, my young people get made fun of at school. The other kids say things like, "Oh, you go to that church where they flop like fish out of water." And my kids don't even bat an eye. They just square their shoulders and say, "Yeah, that's right. Why don't you come and flop with us?" My kids just don't care. Reverend Leonard Ravenhill, once said, "A man who is intimate with God is not intimidated by people."

Well, I said to that principal and her teachers, "Listen. Do me a favor. Don't touch them; just leave them alone and watch them to see if there is a change in their lives."

One of the teachers came up to me months later and told me about one of those kids. "Last year," she said, "that boy was in detention half the time. This year he has not been in detention once."

I don't understand why many people shake and fall in the presence of God. But when I hear stories like that it doesn't matter to me how God moves. I say, "Hey, God, whenever, however, You want to do it, I'll be there. I'll go to the schools. I'll go to the malls. I'll go to the convenience stores and clean up the mess as long as You keep changing lives. You just go ahead and do whatever You want to do."

And I tell my young people constantly, "If God is using you, let God use you. But if you *ever* coerce something or try to make something up, I will be the first one to blast you."

There is a Christian school in our area that takes a strong stand against us. If one of the teachers were to come to the revival they would be fired. That school disagrees completely with this revival. I used to have six of their students in my youth meetings; now we have over 30. There is one girl who has been such a headache to that school. She graduated this year, and they are so relieved. In that school you are not supposed to talk about the Holy Ghost or speaking in tongues or backsliding, but Megan just didn't care. She would tell it like it is, and she got suspended more than once for her bold stand.

One morning before their first class Megan and the other kids who come to our youth meetings joined hands and prayed for their school. The power of God fell and they started shaking. That is a no-no on that campus. A lot of the other students began making fun of them.

The principal called Megan in because she is usually the ringleader. "Megan," he said, "shut the door. I want you to understand right now that what happened here this morning will never happen again." Megan just knew she was about to be suspended again.

He said, "I am talking to you now as your friend and not your principal. What happened will never happen again. I will never again allow the students of this school to make fun of you."

He said, "I want to thank you, Megan, because I have finally met some teenagers who really live what they believe."

Campus ministries are our biggest thrust into the community. We encourage our kids to "go public" with their faith on the front lawn. Several campus ministries outgrew their classrooms this year and had to move to band rooms, choir halls, and gymnasiums because of the crowds. During the 1995 school year, our kids brought 1,000 young people as first-time guests to our youth services. This was in addition to the out of town visitors. We have an average of 20 to 30 visitors from the local community every week.

Follow-up of newcomers is handled like this:

- We ask first-time visitors from the local area to a brief reception right then and there at our youth meeting. We feed them, which is a great start to a relationship with teens; then we ask them to fill out a guest form.

- On our guest forms we ask them what church they go to and who their pastor is. Some people will say they go to a certain church, but if they can't even tell me the pastor's name, I follow them up. If they are definitely from another church, we leave them alone.

- When a teen responds to the altar call, they are prayed with, then introduced to some members of a discipleship group. My kids know that when they meet someone at the altar, that means they have the ball. They befriend the person.

- The goal is to get this new person into discipleship. After a preliminary conversation, my teens say, "Hey, would you like to join our discipleship group? The only problem is that we are in the third week; you won't be able to graduate with us, but here, I'll show you something. They take the new person off to the side and go through lesson #1 of our devotional book with him and then give it to him so he can keep going.

* My kids then call the new person every day or two to check on him. They call their leader and report how the new person is doing. Then, when we pass out applications for the next session of discipleship, this new person signs up because he knows that this is what it is all about; he's learned that this is how it is supposed to be.

In addition to the weekly campus ministries, we do an average of two evening youth rallies in area schools every month, which are student led and student initiated. They publicize we are going to be there, and we hold the rally in the school gym or auditorium. We have testimonies, and our youth band leads some praise and worship. Let me tell you, teenagers listen to teenagers. When they see light radiating from someone their own age, it hits them. Hundreds of young people have been reached through these rallies.

As youth pastor of Brownsville Assembly, I receive a constant flood of speaking invitations. I could be traveling full time. God hasn't called me to that. He has told me that there are a lot of youth evangelists and preachers who are better speakers than me, and I am to stay home. The Lord has released me to speak at youth pastors' conferences, but my first responsibility is to the youth here in our area and to set standards in revival. I do not take lightly what God has given me to do.

By writing this book, I will be able to speak to people without leaving home. What I have had to say is simple. I am not a big hot shot with all the answers. I am just in the right place at the right time. The very fact that I am not a fancy big-name guy should in itself motivate you. When God measures a man or woman, He puts the tape around their heart, not around their head.

It is my heart's desire that something in this book has given you some hope; that something has helped inspire vision and direction in your ministry to today's teenagers. It is summed up with the greatest commandment: Love the Lord your God with all your heart, soul, mind, and strength; and love your neighbor as yourself. Love God and love teenagers. Period.

Conclusion

Saving the Best Until Last

Most everyone you talk to today believes that we are living in the last days. As we draw close to the year 2000 and technology continues to escalate, even the most blatant of sinners have a sense of urgency that the world, as we know it, is about to come to an end. Tension is building. Fear is growing more intense. People's hearts are failing them because of the pressures of life that continue to surmount on a daily basis.

Surely the Scriptures are true when they proclaim "that in the last days perilous times shall come" (2 Tim. 3:1). This is the worst time in the history of man that one could be born because of the wickedness and evil that abounds in our day.

However, it is also the greatest day in which one could live if he or she knows and walks in the anointing of Holy Spirit. For also in the last days God has promised, "I will pour out of My Spirit upon all flesh: and your sons and your daughters shall prophesy, and your young men shall see visions, and your old men shall dream dreams" (Acts 2:17). His Word also declares that "where sin abounded, grace did much more abound" (Rom. 5:20).

Throughout history, every time that satan would raise his ugly head and try to destroy man, the Lord has always been faithful to raise up a standard against him. God has always had a champion in the making who would step forward at just the right time to destroy the very powers of darkness.

Most of the time this champion would not be recognized by those who were around him until he had already won the victory! When David took lunch out to his brothers on that day of battle, nobody recognized him as the mighty giant killer. In fact, he was ridiculed by his brothers and was told to return home. Only after he came back to camp holding Goliath's head did they all start to sing his praises.

This is the case with almost every great champion of the Lord.

Satan was often the only one who knew that a champion was soon to arise on the scene and he would do anything in his power to destroy them before they could grow up and bring him doom.

Remember when the children of Israel were in bondage and God was going to raise up a deliverer named Moses. What did satan do? He had the government leader, Pharaoh, put out a decree to destroy all the baby boys. But God supernaturally delivered Moses, and Moses grew up to become the great deliverer for Israel.

When Jesus, our Great Deliverer, was being born, do you remember what satan did? He had the government leader, Herod, put out a decree throughout the land to destroy all of the baby boys. But God once again delivered Jesus, and Jesus grew up to become the Lamb of God who sets the captives free.

I believe that once again God has been preparing not just one champion, but a whole generation of champions. Generation X—the throw-away generation, the rebellious, confused, hopeless kids you see all around you are America's greatest hope. And just as before, satan has had the government officials put out a decree throughout the land on January 22, 1973—we know it as Roe versus Wade. This decree says to kill all of the babies. We call it abortion, but God calls it murder. However, God has delivered them once again, and we are going to see them rise up in mighty victory and win back our land.

Many of you probably enjoy sports. There are some things that we can learn about the day we are living in from a game of sports. Have you ever noticed how relaxed everybody is at the beginning of a game? If your team scores on the first shot in a basketball game you don't jump up and down like some lunatic. If you did, everyone around you would think you were nuts and wish they weren't sitting near you. However, as the game comes to a close and time becomes short, the tension builds in the air and everybody is standing on their feet and going bananas whenever their team scores. It is the same in life. Everything in life is growing more intense on a daily basis as we draw near to the end of time.

Hear are some other lessons that we must learn about the end of the game.

First, at the end of a game every play is critical. As we draw nigh to the end of time, we must recognize that we do not have time or energy to waste and that we must make the most of every opportunity given us today. For today is the day of salvation. We aren't guaranteed tomorrow. We aren't guaranteed another shot, or another chance. The time is critical, and the time is now!

Second, the pressure at the end of the game separates the champs from the chumps. Many who want to do great things for God are going to wimp out in these last days as the pressure increases. There is a separation coming to the Church. Some will rise up as champions; others will fall out of the game.

Third, the coach always plays his best available players at the end of the game. You never see a coach play the second or third string players at the end of a close, important game. He always uses his best! I believe God knew every one of us before the very foundation of the world was laid and He determined long before He created Adam who would live during different periods of time. And just as a coach wants his best available players in the game at the end, likewise the Lord has hand-picked this generation, a chosen generation, to come in at the end of the game to bring the victory home!

Notice though, the coach can only use the best available players. Sometimes the best players are not available at the end of the game because they have committed too many fouls and thus have become disqualified. Many whom God has chosen will not be able to enjoy the pleasure of winning the victory because they disqualified themselves by playing around with sin. I plead with you, my friend; don't be disqualified. Rather, live holy and make yourself available for the Master's use.

Fourth, the coach always saves his time-outs for the end of the game. There are two reasons for this: one, to pull his players out of the heat of the game and give them a pep talk; two, to plan out the next play with his team. As we draw near to the end of time, it is crucial that we covet our quiet time with God. It is important that we take time to come out of the battle of life and listen to God's game plan for the day and allow Him to give us a good pep talk!

One last observation: At the end of an important game, the real champions will continue to play hard even when wounded and tired. Often we can become weak and want to sit on the bench for a while and allow someone else to carry the load, but as champions, this is no time to rest. It is a time to fight harder than ever before. When Jesus comes there will be plenty of time to rest. But for now, let us fight the good fight, let us keep the faith; let us continue to press forward in Christ Jesus. Let us win, build, and send a whole generation of champions into the battlefield for our Lord.

The world will soon stand to its feet and cheer as God's hidden champions step forward at the close of this century to score the winning goal.

It's time!

Appendix

Talking to the Brownsville Teens

JANET

DESTINY IMAGE: How long have you been coming to the Brownsville church?

JANET: I came for the first time the Sunday after Father's Day 1995. My cousin, who we all call Aunt Linda, is my youth pastor at our Methodist church, and she brought our whole youth group here that Sunday night.

DESTINY IMAGE: What happened to you that night?

JANET: I have been raised in church all my life, but I didn't know God. Church was just something you did on Sunday for an hour. At home and church I was like Little Miss Perfect, but at school I was totally another way. I had a filthy mouth. I cussed the wallpaper off the wall, it was so bad.

DESTINY IMAGE: You could cuss the wallpaper off the wall?

JANET: Yeah. And I was in gymnastics for 14 years and I'm pretty strong physically. I have a twin brother, John, and he's 6'3" tall. He's like a tree or something. I used to pick fights at school and on the bus. I was a bully. I picked fights with boys or girls all the time. Then if I couldn't take them, my brother would take them for me 'cause he was just as bad as I was.

DESTINY IMAGE: So what happened that first night you went to church at Brownsville?

JANET: We walked in the door and there were people all over the floor. I was not raised that way. The Methodists didn't do that. I said to my youth pastor, "Aunt Linda, why are all those people on the floor?" And she said it was the Holy Spirit. And I said, "Who's that?" I never knew about Him. Aunt Linda had always taught the Word to us. We used to call her the "living Bible." She taught us, but we never paid any attention to what she was saying.

Well, I watched this guy Steve Hill putting his hands on people's foreheads and they were falling over and stuff. Aunt Linda explained that the Holy Spirit is like lightning, and we are like transformers; and once God hits us, then we can send it out to other people. I said, "Well, I'm not one of them. Keep him away from me."

DESTINY IMAGE: Were you afraid?

JANET: No. But I got scared on Wednesday night. My brother got prayed for that night. Steve Hill prayed for him and he fell down right at my feet. I screamed and ran as fast as I could. My brother just does not do that. I was totally scared. Aunt Linda came running after me, and I said, "I want to go home. I want to go home now. Get me out of here." They told me I couldn't because the rest of the youth group was still there.

They dragged me back to Steve Hill. I said, "Please don't touch me." He just took my hand; he was really gentle. He seemed to look right into me. It was like he could see every sin I had ever committed. He said, "I'm just going to pray that God blesses you." I nodded OK, and then boom—I hit the floor.

I heard God talk to me. It was like He said, "I'm sick of your pride. I'm sick of your attitude. Choose who you are going to serve." He said, "I've had My hand on you all your life. Your youth pastor has prayed for you since you were little. Decide right now who you are going to serve—the devil or Me."

Then it was like He hit me with a two by four. I woke up 45 minutes later and I was totally wasted. I was drunk. I was walking crooked. My eyes were glazed.

For the next three weeks I got Steve to pray for me six times a night. I just couldn't get enough of Jesus after that one time. People carried me out night after night. I would drive to church but somebody else had to drive me home every night.

DESTINY IMAGE: What did your family think of what was happening?

JANET: That first night we got home at 6:30 a.m. and the sun was coming up. We had been at church almost 12 hours. And my mom was like, "Where have you been? Have you been with Linda? You better have been with Linda." She couldn't believe it. I had never wanted to go to church before. I had always said I was sick on Sundays. She called Linda, and sure enough I had been at church all that time. That's how my mom got into it.

DESTINY IMAGE: Are you still part of the Methodist youth group?

JANET: Yes. I am the president this year.

DESTINY IMAGE: Are there a lot of changes among the kids?

JANET: Yes. We are so on fire for God.

DESTINY IMAGE: What is helping you the most?

JANET: Prayer. Seven days a week there is a prayer group at our church. And our youth group is growing so much and people know if they want to come to our youth group, they'd better be spiritual. And Brother Richard's discipleship program is helping. It's great. There are Baptists, Lutherans, Catholics, and Methodists in discipleship. It's a lot of fun 'cause we do not really care about what church we go to.

DESTINY IMAGE: If you had the chance to talk to youth pastors, what would you say to them?

JANET: I would tell them to keep praying for their youth; and I would tell them to preach the truth. Preach the truth. Teenagers are sick of religion. We're sick of going to church and leaving the same way we came every Sunday. We are hungry for God; and we're hungry for His power.

Brother Richard tells the truth. And I can talk to him about anything. With my dad being away from God, it's good to have a spiritual father, a human father. I can go to Brother Richard and say, "This is what I'm going through. What do I do?" And I know he will tell me the truth.

JOHN

DESTINY IMAGE: John, you are Janet's twin brother. Tell me what happened to you.

JOHN: Well, I was saved, but I was kinda backslidden. I went to church because my mom made me. The first night I came to Brownsville, my cousin's daughter, Lydia, asked me if I would go forward for prayer. I figured it couldn't hurt, so I went down to the front. Steve Hill walked up to me and looked right at me with his eyes, and I kinda pushed Lydia in front of me. I was scared. Then he turned and prayed for some other guys. I gave this sigh of relief. Then I looked down and there was Lydia lying on the floor. He hadn't touched her or anything.

Then Steve came back and asked if I wanted to get prayed for. I said sure, but I didn't think I would fall down. He said, "You just do whatever the Lord tells you to do." So I was getting prayed for. I didn't know what to do, so I just closed my eyes. Then I felt this weight just come on top of me. I tried to stay up; I really tried. Then it felt like this wind or wave just came and took out my legs. People told me I jumped up and flopped down. I don't remember. I just know my life changed, and I have never been the same since.

DESTINY IMAGE: What changed in your life?

JOHN: The way I looked at going to church. After that I *wanted* to go to church. I was at church almost every day; I just wanted to go there. I listened to the sermons and actually took in what was said. And my music changed. I listen to the Christian station now. I have gone from running with gang members to hanging out with friends who are Christians.

The biggest change in my life is that before, I knew Jesus and I could tell you a lot about Him; but now He has become my best friend. I have learned to talk to Him as if He were sitting right here. Sometimes when I am alone and I have trouble concentrating or something, I just sit back and say, "Look, Jesus, You know, this is my problem...."

ASHLEY

DESTINY IMAGE: Ashley, you were already part of Brownsville when the revival started. What did you think about what was happening to your church?

ASHLEY: I remember looking around and thinking, "This is really strange. I have never seen people act like this. They are so alive." I had grown up in church all my life but July 6, 1995, I really got to know the Lord. I went to the altar and cried and shook. It was a really good feeling. It was like I was being released. God has completely blessed me since the revival.

DESTINY IMAGE: Do you have any brothers or sisters?

ASHLEY: I have an eight-year-old sister and a six-year-old brother. They get into a lot of fights when I'm watching them. Sending them out of the room doesn't seem to work. The best thing I can do, and it really gets them to shut their mouths, is to tell them exactly what it says in the Bible. When they hit each other, I tell them the Bible says you should not lay your hands upon your brother or sister unless you are blessing them. I say, "Now, were you blessing her?" "No." "Then you keep your hands off of her." It works.

DESTINY IMAGE: Ashley, if you could give advice to youth pastors, considering what Brother Richard has done right to help you kids, what would you say?

ASHLEY: I would say to spend as much time with your kids as you can and pour your soul into them, because they are the next generation and that's how you are going to make it with your youth. That will make them closer to God when they see you and how you are living. And when you spend so much time with them they see all the love in you.

DESTINY IMAGE: The revival is two years old now. You are still walking strong and still loving the Lord. What has helped you do that?

ASHLEY: Discipleship. I have an accountability partner. That is the person you talk to every week. I am also accountable to my best friends. They know everything about me, and I know everything about them. And memorizing all the verses helps a lot. If I get scared or hurt, if I'm fixing to lose it, I quote a Scripture and it helps to calm me down a lot to know that God is with me.

DESTINY IMAGE: Ashley, friends are very important to teenagers. What has happened to your friendships since the revival?

ASHLEY: We all became more friendly; there is love in the friendship now. We don't get upset about every little thing. But my friends at school have grown more distant because now I stand strong and won't back down.

I was talking to some girls one day about church, and they are all pretty bad girls, and one said, "Is that where the Holy Spirit falls on you and you kinda shake a little bit and you fall in the Spirit and God blesses you and everything?" The word has gotten around and they know who we are and they are watching us. That's another thing that keeps me going. I'm being watched. If I should fall, I would bring disgrace to my God's face.

JENNIFER

DESTINY IMAGE: Jennifer, you are 17 years old, and God uses you powerfully in intercession. As you are going around the room praying for people here in

Brownsville, I've watched you trembling and crying; I've seen the Holy Spirit resting on you. Can you tell what's going on in you as you pray? How do you feel?

JENNIFER: I don't really understand all the details. But it's like...if somebody is hurting inside and wants to cry, I start crying. I am wailing and crying and before you know it, they start wailing and crying. It's like I sometimes do the breaking through for them, like I'm standing in the gap or something.

DESTINY IMAGE: That is exactly what you are doing. Then what happens?

JENNIFER: Then God takes over. I love praying for people because I love the way God works. It is so awesome. I never experienced it before. Sometimes I feel the joy in people that is ready to bust. I intercede for them and laugh at the same time. Then it breaks and they start laughing and laughing. It's so much fun!

DESTINY IMAGE: Jennifer, you grew up in church. If you could say something to other teenagers with a similar background as yours, what would you say?

JENNIFER: I would say what Steve Hill says: "Stop hanging *around* the cross and get *on* the cross." Lay down your life for Jesus. He died for you—why can't you live for Him?

KENZIE

DESTINY IMAGE: Kenzie, I heard that you are here at the church "all the time." Tell me what has happened in your life to make you want to hang out at church?

KENZIE: I wasn't really a horrible heathen, but there is no such thing as big or little sin. I would get with my friends and we would drink and party and I am only 13 years old. I was sitting on my bed one night and the conviction of the Holy Spirit just came over me, and I was like, "What am I doing?" This is so stupid. I am on the verge of destruction here. And I just went on a rampage through my room.

I broke all my CDs and threw out all my pictures. Most of the pictures were from before I got saved, and I just don't want to remember those days. Especially after I got baptized, 'cause when you get baptized you are dying to your old self and coming up renewed. Why would I want to remember my old life?

DESTINY IMAGE: Have other people seen a change in you?

KENZIE: My school is just so awesome seeing how people are reacting. I love persecution. I get cussed out and they say stuff like, "Instead of saying we're going to hell, why don't you just say we're not going to Heaven?" Hell is not fun and games, and I am not going to candy coat it.

People have said that our generation is going downhill. That might be true in some cases, but here at Brownsville, we are going to take over this generation. I know we are. It won't be us; it will be the Holy Spirit working through us. I am giving all the glory to God. I always pray for Jesus to open the doors so I can witness to people, and I just pray for Him to give me the words to speak. He speaks through me.

DESTINY IMAGE: Kenzie, why do you think you are on the earth? What is the point of being here?

KENZIE: I think the point of being here is to share the gospel and to live for Jesus, and we are made to worship Him. It makes me so mad when Christians go out and do other stuff.

The other night my friend and I called this girl in our discipleship group who had been missing a lot of days. When we called, she was having a party at her house. We could hear the music in the background. There were other people there who were supposed to be Christians and none of them wanted to talk to us. They were drinking and doing stuff they shouldn't be doing. I don't care if they were sitting there and not drinking or anything. If they were in that house, they were in sin.

My friend, Jill, and I started praying and we asked my Aunt Mary if she would drive us over to that house. When we got there people were all over the yard smoking cigarettes. We parked the car and kept on praying. Two or three carloads left. People just started scattering. Then the music was off—no more loud music. And then we saw two of the girls we had really been praying for outside crying because they were under conviction. If that wasn't the Holy Spirit, I don't know what is. It was awesome. We were like, whoa, thank You, Jesus!

DESTINY IMAGE: So God is really at work in your friends and at school.

KENZIE: Definitely. It hurts me so bad to go to school and see all that sin. I've had a lot of problems with my friends. They get mad at me because they say I think I'm better than them because I'm a Christian. That's not it at all; you just can't mix good with evil. And I'm not trying to say they are evil or anything, but if they are going to go out and party and drink and do all the stuff they do, how can I be around that and still be a Christian? Evil company corrupts good habits, and I can't have that corrupting my good habits.

DESTINY IMAGE: What has been the most significant thing that has helped you follow Jesus?

KENZIE: I think His love. Your friends will deceive you and hurt you. Your parents might hurt you. People will hurt you but Jesus will never forsake you. It says that in the Bible. And Brother Richard does a good job supporting us. He keeps saying, "Don't get discouraged. Keep going."

JILL

DESTINY IMAGE: Jill, you are Kenzie's friend. Tell me about yourself.

JILL: I used to be really religious, and I thought I was a Christian. My opinion of a Christian was that as long as you go to church and you pray sometimes then you're a Christian. I would lie and cheat and cuss all the time. It was wrong. And I thought I was a Christian. I fooled my parents. I fooled a lot of people. But the Bible says if you are a friend of God, you can't be a friend of the world. You can't serve two masters. And someone had to tell me that.

No one is telling people that at most churches. They are preaching love messages. You know, little "twinkie" messages, and people are satisfied they are going to Heaven. Everything is going to be OK. At Brownsville you get twinkies *and* you get brussel sprouts. Sometimes you've got to feel uncomfortable.

DESTINY IMAGE: When did you make the decision to serve God?

JILL: The summer I was fixing to go into the seventh grade. I had this motivation of winning my whole school for Jesus. When I got to school I lost all my friends, and it was horrible because I had such high expectations. I used to have really close friends who would ask if I wanted to go to the dances and stuff, and I didn't have that desire anymore. I came to church every night and I cried on Brother Richard's shoulder about how I hated it and because I knew it was going to be so hard. Brother Richard was always there for me. Every night he had an encouraging word for me. But I had to go through it. I believe it was an endurance test that God put me through. I went a whole year without anybody getting saved. Then the next summer my friends started getting saved, like Kenzie for instance.

DESTINY IMAGE: That was the summer of 1996?

JILL: Yes. And at the beginning of the school year I went to my principal and she finally said OK for us to start a Bible ministry. It's not some cute little Bible club; we preach the Word. We tell them going to church will not save you. If you do not have a personal relationship with Jesus, you are going to hell. We meet in the computer room now and have about 50 to 60 people. People get saved every week. And we give them Bibles.

DESTINY IMAGE: Who prays with them to accept the Lord?

JILL: I do. They raise their hand for salvation and then come to the front. It's a public thing. Kids are getting on fire for God and praying for their families. One girl prayed for her grandfather and he got healed of cancer. God is really moving.

ROBBIE

DESTINY IMAGE: Robbie, I heard that God is also really moving at your school.

ROBBIE: Yeah. And I wear a suit and tie to school now.

Everybody calls me a preacher. Two of my friends and I started carrying our Bibles around and talking to people about Jesus and then we started praying at lunch time. There are 50 of us who pray at lunch time now.

BONNIE

BONNIE: This girl, Gretchen, came to my school. I had known her for four days, and she said the Lord sent her there because someone needed the Lord. It was me. One day the Holy Spirit came on her and she was shaking. It was really awesome. She gave me a tract to read and I read it right then and there. I read it again when I got home. I took my Bible with me to school the next day. It was time to make a change. I said to her, "Let's go to Bible class." I thank the Lord for sending Gretchen to my school.

ERIC

DESTINY IMAGE: Eric, tell me what the discipleship program here at Brownsville has done for you.

ERIC: I'm in my fourth term now. They separate you into groups and put somebody above you. You are accountable to that person and they make sure you are reading your Bible and praying and memorizing Scripture and fasting one meal a week and witnessing to at least one person.

One thing I had to ask for was boldness to witness. Carrying your Bible around at school is not a popular thing to do and I lost all my friends. I lost all my friends and I didn't have much to do so I started going to the library and reading my Bible. That was cool. People started asking me a lot of questions.

The Bible says to go into all the world and preach the gospel. I don't remember Jesus saying, "Please go preach the gospel"; or "Do it if you want to." No, He said to do it. Ezekiel 3 says if I tell a wicked man about his sins then I'm not held accountable. I realized that if I don't witness to the kids at school, I *will* be held accountable. For a while, I was the only Christian. There are 15 of us carrying our Bibles around the school now.

DESTINY IMAGE: How old are you?

ERIC: I'm 15.

DESTINY IMAGE: You have two more years of school. What are you expecting to happen?

ERIC: I have a vision of people falling under conviction at our school and the teachers singing praise and worship songs in the classrooms. I can't wait for the power of God to hit kids and throw them against their lockers. It's going to be awesome.

EMILY

DESTINY IMAGE: Emily, what has changed in your life since the revival?

EMILY: I was a brat. I was so stuck up that if I said hi to someone in the hall at school I would think that person was really privileged because I said hi to them. It was disgusting. I hate to think that I was ever that way.

I went to the same school for eight years. Everybody knew me. The teachers and principal knew me. All the kids knew me. After God touched me and I got right with Him, everybody was like, "What happened to you??" I felt like I was going to bust. I just could not talk about God enough. I could not get it out of my system. I still can't. I still cannot talk about God enough. I preach all the time and they hate me because I preach all the time. I've even had death threats. It's kinda cool.

JONATHAN

DESTINY IMAGE: Jonathan, you were 16 years old when the revival broke out. What happened to you?

JONATHAN: It was the third Friday night after it started. I was on the stage playing my trombone. Charity was singing and Steve Hill was talking about how religion is hanging *around* the cross and Christianity is getting *on* the cross. He had said that before, but it didn't sink in until then. I started thinking about it. I knew how to do everything, what to say, and I was pretty decent; but I didn't have the relationship that I should have had. So I went down to the altar. It was pretty tough going down there from being on the stage, but it was awesome. I got prayed for over and over again because there was like a wall there.

About 10:00 p.m. I got prayed for the seventh time. I said, "Lord, I want to get on the cross with You." He said, "Are you sure?" I said, "Yes." And He said, "Are you sure?" And I said "Yes." And He said, "OK." And it was like I went through everything He went through. I didn't feel the pain, but I felt the humility and the shame. I know it's not even close, but I felt a little bit of what He felt like. It was enough for me and for the first time I realized what Jesus had done for me. I had gone to church all my life, but I had never realized how much He loved me and what He really did; what all He went through. And it completely changed me. He has cleaned me out.

D *Destiny Image*
Revival Books

WHEN THE HEAVENS ARE BRASS
by John Kilpatrick.

Pastor John Kilpatrick wanted something more. He began to pray, but it seemed like the heavens were brass. The lessons he learned over the years helped birth a mighty revival in Brownsville Assembly of God that is sweeping through this nation and the world. The dynamic truths in this book could birth life-changing revival in your own life and ministry!

Paperback Book, 168p. ISBN 1-56043-190-3 (6" X 9") Retail $9.99

WHITE CANE RELIGION
And Other Messages From the Brownsville Revival
by Stephen Hill.

In less than two years, Evangelist Stephen Hill has won nearly 100,000 to Christ while preaching repentance, forgiveness, and the power of the blood in what has been called "The Brownsville Revival" in Pensacola, Florida. Experience the anointing of the best of this evangelist's life-changing revival messages in this dynamic book!

Paperback Book, 182p. ISBN 1-56043-186-5 Retail $9.99

PORTAL IN PENSACOLA
by Renee DeLoriea.

What is happening in Pensacola, Florida? Why are people from all over the world streaming to one church in this city? The answer is simple: ***Revival!*** For more than a year, Renee DeLoriea has lived in the midst of the revival at Brownsville Assembly of God. *Portal in Pensacola* is her firsthand account of this powerful move of the Spirit that is illuminating and transforming the lives of thousands!

Paperback Book, 182p. ISBN 1-56043-189-X Retail $9.99

Destiny Image
Revival Books

THE GOD MOCKERS
And Other Messages From the Brownsville Revival
by Stephen Hill.
Hear the truth of God as few men have dared to tell it! In his usual passionate and direct manner, Evangelist Stephen Hill directs people to an uncompromised Christian life of holiness. The messages in this book will burn through every hindrance that keeps you from going further in God!
Paperback Book, 182p. ISBN 1-56043-691-3 Retail $9.99

CHILDREN OF REVIVAL
by Vann Lane.
What do you do with hundreds of children during services that last for hours? At first Pastor Vann Lane thought he would use all his usual "stuff" to entertain the children. The Lord thought differently. In this book you'll read remarkable stories of Brownsville Assembly's 11-year-old leader, the worship band of young musicians, and the 75-member prayer team of children between ages 8 and 12 years old. *Children of Revival* will forever change the way you view the Church's little members.
Paperback Book, 144p. ISBN 1-56043-699-9 Retail $9.99

LET NO ONE DECEIVE YOU
by Dr. Michael L. Brown.
No one is knowingly deceived. Everyone assumes it's "the other guy" who is off track. So when people dispute the validity of current revivals, how do you know who is right? In this book Dr. Michael Brown takes a look at current revivals and at the arguments critics are using to question their validity. After examining Scripture, historical accounts of past revivals, and the fruits of the current movements, Dr. Brown comes to a logical conclusion: God's Spirit is moving. *Let No One Deceive You!*
Paperback Book, 320p. ISBN 1-56043-693-X (6" X 9") Retail $10.99

A TOUCH OF GLORY
by Lindell Cooley.
This book was written for the countless "unknowns" who, like Lindell Cooley, are being plucked from obscurity for a divine work of destiny. Here Lindell, the worship leader of the Brownsville Revival, tells of his own journey from knowing God's hand was upon him to trusting Him. The key to personal revival is a life-changing encounter with the living God. There is no substitute for a touch of His glory.
Paperback Book, 182p. ISBN 1-56043-689-1 Retail $9.99

Available at your local Christian bookstore.

Internet: http://www.reapernet.com

Prices subject to change without notice.

Destiny Image
Revival Books

HIS MANIFEST PRESENCE

by Don Nori.

This is a passionate look at God's desire for a people with whom He can have intimate fellowship. Not simply a book on worship, it faces our triumphs as well as our sorrows in relation to God's plan for a dwelling place that is splendid in holiness and love.

Paperback Book, 182p. ISBN 0-914903-48-9 Retail $8.99

PRAYER AND FASTING

by Dr. Kingsley Fletcher.

We cry, "O God...bring revival to our families, our churches, and our nation." But we end our prayers quickly—everyone is hungry and we must eat before our food gets cold. Is it any wonder that our prayers are not prevailing? Discover the benefits of prayer and fasting...and learn to fast successfully.

Paperback Book, 168p. ISBN 1-56043-070-2 Retail $9.99

REQUIREMENTS FOR GREATNESS

by Lori Wilke.

Everyone longs for greatness, but do we know what God's requirements are? In this life-changing message, Lori Wilke shows how Jesus exemplified true greatness, and how we must take on His attributes of justice, mercy, and humility to attain that greatness in His Kingdom.

Paperback Book, 182p. ISBN 1-56043-152-0 Retail $9.99

SECRETS OF THE MOST HOLY PLACE

by Don Nori.

Here is a prophetic parable you will read again and again. The winds of God are blowing, drawing you to His Life within the Veil of the Most Holy Place. There you begin to see as you experience a depth of relationship your heart has yearned for. This book is a living, dynamic experience with God!

Paperback Book, 182p. ISBN 1-56043-076-1 Retail $9.99

Available at your local Christian bookstore.

Internet: http://www.reapernet.com

Prices subject to change without notice.

Destiny Image
New Releases

WHEN GOD STRIKES THE MATCH
by Dr. Harvey R. Brown, Jr.
A noted preacher, college administrator, and father of an "all-American" family—what more could a man want? But when God struck the match that set Harvey Brown ablaze, it ignited a passion for holiness and renewal in his heart that led him into a head-on encounter with the consuming fire of God.
Paperback Book, 160p. ISBN 0-7684-1000-2 (6" X 9") Retail $9.99

THE LOST ART OF INTERCESSION
by Jim W. Goll.
How can you experience God's anointing power as a result of your own prayer? Learn what the Moravians discovered during their 100-year prayer Watch. They sent up prayers; God sent down His power. Jim Goll, who ministers worldwide through a teaching and prophetic ministry, urges us to heed Jesus' warning to "watch." Through Scripture, the Moravian example, and his own prayer life, Jim Goll proves that "what goes up must come down."
Paperback Book, 182p. ISBN 1-56043-697-2 Retail $9.99

WORSHIP: THE PATTERN OF THINGS IN HEAVEN
by Joseph L. Garlington.
Joseph Garlington, a favorite Promise Keepers' speaker and worship leader, delves into Scripture to reveal worship and praise from a Heaven's-eye view. Learn just how deep, full, and anointed God intends our worship to be.
Paperback Book, 182p. ISBN 1-56043-195-4 Retail $9.99

Available at your local Christian bookstore.

Internet: http://www.reapernet.com

Prices subject to change without notice.